Turmoil in the Middle East

Imperialism, War, and Political Instability

Berch Berberoglu

STATE UNIVERSITY OF NEW YORK PRESS

Published by
State University of New York Press

© 1999 Berch Berberoglu

Printed in the United States of America

For information, address the State University of New York Press,
State University Plaza, Albany, NY 12246

Marketing by Patrick Durocher • Production by Bernadine Dawes

Library of Congress Cataloging-in-Publication Data

Berberoglu, Berch.
    Turmoil in the Middle East : imperialism, war, and political
  instability / Berch Berberoglu.
        p.   cm.
    Includes bibliographical references (p.   ) and index.
    ISBN 0-7914-4411-2 (hc : alk. paper). — ISBN 0-7914-4412-0 (pb :
  alk. paper)
    1. Middle East—Politics and government—20th century. 2. Middle
  East—Social conditions—20th century. 3. Imperialism. I. Title.
  DS62.8.B44   1999
    956.04—DC21   99-13221
                                                            CIP

1   2   3   4   5   6   7   8   9   10

*Turmoil
in the
Middle East*

Dedicated to

the memory of

my grandfather,

"Dede"

CONTENTS

PREFACE

This project has been in the making for nearly a decade. In a previous book, *Power and Stability in the Middle East*, I showed the lack of any lasting stability in this war-torn region of the world. The present book was conceived as a sequel to this work to highlight the impact of imperialism, war, and political turmoil in the Middle East throughout the course of the twentieth century—from the devastation of the First World War through the many crises and conflicts that have led to cycles of war, uprisings, coups, revolts, and revolutions.

This book has benefited from several visits to the Middle East over the past number of years, including Turkey, Egypt, Syria, Cyprus, Greece, Armenia, Morocco, Tunisia, Lebanon, Israel, and the West Bank. My latest visits to the region— Greece and Armenia in 1995, Cyprus and Lebanon in 1996, Cyprus, Egypt, Israel, and the West Bank in 1997, Lebanon in 1998, and Greece in 1999—have allowed me the opportunity to deliver a series of lectures and meet with colleagues at several universities, including the American University of Beirut, the Lebanese American University, the Haigazian University College, the American University in Cairo, the University of Cyprus, the American University of Armenia, the American College of Thessaloniki, and the Center for Asia Minor Studies. Colleagues and friends at these and other universities and research centers throughout the Middle East have provided much valuable information, which I have incorporated into this book.

While the book focuses on the internal contradictions of Middle Eastern states driven by the dynamics of class conflict and class struggle in various realms of society and social relations, the political economy of long-embedded conflicts and crises in the Middle East are examined with special attention to the role of powerful, external forces stemming from Western imperialism led by Britain, France, and later the United States.

The centrality of the relationship between imperialism, war, and political turmoil in the Middle East is shown in this book with particular reference to an analysis of the class nature of the state, the social forces involved in nationalist and fundamentalist movements, and the organizational context in which these forces are politically mobilized to effect change. Thus, the collapse of the Ottoman state, the emergence of the newly formed nation-states, the struggles of the Palestinians, Kurds, and other national minorities, the civil wars and regional conflicts and wars, including the Arab-Israeli conflict and the Gulf War, as well as the many uprisings, rebellions, and revolutions—from the Palestinian and Kurdish revolts of the 1930s to the revolution in Iran to the Intifada in the Occupied Territories—are all examined within the framework of a class-analysis approach that takes into account the central role of imperialism and neo-colonial reaction as the twin pillars of the contemporary world political economy that have impacted the Middle East.

It is a difficult task to sort out the class forces that underlie the political conflicts that have led to civil strife and military confrontation throughout the Middle East. Providing an analysis of the class nature of the state and the balance of class forces involved in struggle for political supremacy across much of the Middle East, this book attempts to map out the dynamics of social change and social transformation in this turbulent—and vitally important—region of the world.

ACKNOWLEDGMENTS

Examining within the confines of a small book the depth and breadth of a century of historic events that have left their mark on an entire region such as the Middle East is not an easy task. The information and analysis provided in the following pages is the result of the work of dozens of scholars and specialists of the Middle East that I have examined over many years of research and writing; in the process, I have developed my own perspective, which has served as the basis for an understanding of social, economic, and political structures and institutions that define the nature and dynamics of the contemporary Middle East.

In this effort, many colleagues and students have contributed, directly or indirectly, to the shaping of my views on matters dealing with the crucial issues raised and discussed in this book. I would like to thank Vahakn Dadrian, Cyrus Bina, Sohrab Behdad, Fikret Ceyhun, Amir Soltani, Savvas Katsikides, Asef Bayat, and Levon Vartan for their contribution to discussions on the nature and dynamics of major events in the Middle East.

I would like to thank Clay Morgan and Zina Lawrence, my editors at SUNY Press, for allowing me the additional time I needed to complete this project and for their patience and cooperation through various stages of the publication process.

The research effort that went into the preparation of this manuscript was made possible by a grant from the University of Nevada, Reno Foundation. It was awarded as part of my Foundation Professorship from 1995 to 1998, which provided me the necessary funds and the release time needed to complete this project.

Finally, I would like to thank my wife, Suzan, for her many years of companionship and encouragement of my work, and for providing valuable commentary and criticism that has enriched my analysis at every turn; and to thank my sons, Stephen and Michael, for their patience and understanding of the importance of this project.

Introduction

For centuries, the Middle East has been the focal point of imperialist rivalry, war, and political turmoil. The cycles of imperialist incursions into the region have turned this historic corner of the world into a zone of bloodshed and death, destruction and despair.

Interimperialist rivalries have transformed the Middle East into a contested terrain of competing forces vying for control of the territory, culture, and people of this region over the course of the twentieth century. The intrusion of the Western powers into this region facilitated the decline and fall of the Ottoman Empire as a major power in the late nineteenth and early twentieth centuries. The collapse of the Ottoman Empire in turn led to the further expansion of Western imperialism throughout the Middle East.

This book examines the dynamics of social forces behind the political turmoil that has engulfed the contemporary Middle East. Focusing on major political events of the twentieth century, the book explores the origins, nature, and contradictions of conflicts that have turned this region into one of permanent instability.

The opening chapter of this book focuses on the motive force of imperialist expansion into the Middle East beginning in the late nineteenth century and discusses its impact on the region during this period. It shows that the main interest of the Western powers in dominating this region was *oil*. The Baghdad Railway, built by European capital, played a major role in the extraction and distribution of this key resource and became instrumental in assuring the expansion of Western imperialism into this region. This was accompanied by the destruction of native industry in textiles and other sectors of the economy and the subjugation of the local population to the dictates of the Western powers. In sum, the impact of Western imperialism on the Ottoman Empire—and the Middle East in general—was devastating.

Chapter 2 looks at a catastrophic consequence of collapse of the Ottoman Empire during this period of imperialist plunder and destruction: the ultranationalist reaction that led to the massacre of the Armenian people, the first mass genocide of the twentieth century. While other ethnic groups scattered around various corners of the empire succeeded in obtaining their independence and were able to establish a nation-state of their own, the unique situation of Armenians in Turkey during this period prevented them from securing a homeland for themselves. The result for the Armenians was catastrophic: of some 2 million Armenians in Ottoman Turkey, 1.5 million were killed by government orders in a few short years. The fate of the Armenian people in the hands of their Turkish executioners, which was an outcome of the rise to power of the Young Turks at a critical juncture that marked the collapse of the Ottoman Empire, was a prelude to the rise of nationalism and ethnic conflict elsewhere in the Middle East during the course of the twentieth century. While this nationalist upsurge in the old provinces of the Ottoman state engendered an anti-imperialist struggle that led to national independence, this was accomplished not without the repression of ethnic minorities within these national territories, as in the case of the Armenians in Ottoman Turkey and the Kurds in Iraq, Syria, and modern Turkey.

Chapters 3 and 4 provide an analysis of the resurgence of nationalism in the Middle East during the twentieth century. Struggling against the Western occupation of old Ottoman territories, the peoples of Palestine, Egypt, Syria, Lebanon, Iraq, and other regions of the Middle East asserted themselves to gain their independence and to establish a series of nation-states throughout the region by midcentury. Although the leadership of the various national movements that waged war against Western imperialism was made up of an assortment of nationalist forces that were strategically situated in the state bureaucracy—hence the uprisings generally took the form of a military coup, rather than a social revolution—the forces that came to power during this period of nationalist resurgence played an important role in shaping the future course of development of the Middle East in the latter half of the twentieth century. Tracing these developments in four prominent settings in the region, chapter 3 takes up the cases of Turkey and Egypt, and chapter 4 examines the cases of Syria and Iraq—countries that have had, and continue to have, an enormous impact on the entire Middle East.

Chapter 5 addresses the national question in the Middle East, focusing on the Palestinian and Kurdish struggles for national self-determination. It examines the historical experience of the two national/ethnic groups in their efforts to secure a homeland for their people during the course of the twentieth century. Situating this problem in comparative perspective, the national question in the Middle East is addressed as a legacy of Ottoman rule and the post–World War I imperialist policy of territorial division. The intrusion of the Western powers into the Middle East and the occupation and division of the Ottoman territories between the chief imperialist states across the Middle East led to the dispersion of Palestinians and Kurds throughout the region. The partition of the national homeland of the Kurds, the displacement of the Palestinians by the imperialist occupation forces that dominated the region for decades, and the repression of these two national communities by the states that subsequently came to rule over these territories have resulted in the suppression of their legitimate rights to national self-determination. Scattered across several nations in the region, these two groups have been the victims of imperial and national schemes that have relegated them to second-class citizenship in the various states of the Middle East. But, as this chapter documents, the Palestinians and the Kurds are fighting back; they are increasingly politicized and are becoming active in the struggle for independence and national self-determination.

Chapter 6 examines the Arab-Israeli conflict—a conflict stemming from the legacy of Western imperialism. War and political turmoil became the order of the day in the decades following the displacement of the Palestinians and the establishment of the state of Israel in 1948. The British plan to partition Palestine and relinquish other (Arab) territories in the Middle East in the postwar period led to greater conflict in the region as Israel became the sworn enemy of the Arab states, who courted the Palestinian cause in the early years of postcolonial rule throughout the region. The unresolved question of a Palestinian homeland became the rallying point of Arab nationalism that galvanized resentment among Arabs against Israel. This, in turn, led to Israeli reaction directed against both the Arab states and the Palestinian movement in its infancy. Escalating conflict between the two sides led to the Six-Day War of 1967 and to subsequent wars that followed, including the October War of 1973 and the Israeli invasion of Lebanon in 1982.

Chapter 7 focuses on the Gulf War as an outcome of inter-imperialist rivalry between the major imperialist powers over control of oil in the Middle East. Here, it is argued that the rivalry between Japan, Germany, and the United States culminated in a regional power struggle that manifested itself in the Gulf War, but the nature of this competition for domination of the world political economy had deeper roots. As the rising capitalist powers in need of direct access to sources of raw materials, especially oil, Germany and Japan posed a new threat to the United States' traditional hold over the Middle East after the Second World War. The decline in U.S. power in the region in the aftermath of the shah's fall, which allowed the possibility of the emergence of a new regional power center in the Middle East, invited these two emergent centers of world capitalism to play a direct role in the region's changing political economy. The U.S. reaction to this regional power play was quick and swift, culminating in the Gulf War launched by the United States. While its rivals were set back through this action for the time being, the U.S. reentry into the region in the 1990s brought with it a new set of contradictions that, rather than leading to a resolution of the region's problems, actually further intensified them—thus opening the way to renewed conflict and crisis throughout the Middle East.

Finally, chapter 8 discusses the nature of the post–Cold War "New World Order" and considers the prospects for peace in the Middle East in the period ahead.

While developments over the past decade have generated a new dynamic in post-Soviet and post–Cold War politics across the globe, the uncertainties resulting from new rivalries among emerging centers of global power in this most recent period lead us to raise a number of questions regarding the future course of development in the Middle East: Will the Middle East continue to be at the center stage of conflict and crisis as it has been over the past several decades? Or, will a new dynamic emerge and redefine the region's political structure and balance of power in the next decade? Will the persistent Arab-Israeli conflict come to an end once and for all? Or, will new contending forces emerge and consolidate their hold over the masses of both societies to prolong the crisis and plunge the region into further chaos and turmoil?

Providing some provocative answers to these and other related questions, the book concludes its historical analysis of the dynamics of Middle East politics in the current context of the contradictions of the world political economy by rendering an assessment of the prospects for peace and social progress in this volatile region of the world.

1
The Impact of Western Imperialism on the Middle East

Until the beginning of the twentieth century, the major political power in the Middle East was the Ottoman Empire. After centuries of expansion and conquest, the Ottoman state began to lose ground to rival forces in Europe during the eighteenth and nineteenth centuries and became vulnerable to pressures from the West. The Ottoman throne became rapidly weaker and as a consequence its influence in the Mediterranean suffered continual erosion.[1]

With the expansion of European capital to the eastern Mediterranean, in pursuit of raw materials and new markets, commercial ties began to develop between the Ottoman Empire and centers of Western imperialism.[2] Growing trade between Western Europe and Ottoman Turkey during this period began to have adverse effects on local, small-scale Ottoman industry. Faced with rising costs and operating under strict price regulations, the Ottoman guilds were unable to provide goods at prices low enough to compete with the cheap manufactured goods from Europe that entered the empire without restriction.[3] Consequently, traditional Ottoman industry entered a period of rapid decline and the empire became more and more tied to and dependent on the European economies.

The process of British (and other European) expansion into the Ottoman economy accelerated following the Anglo-Turkish Commercial Convention of 1838, which extended extraterritorial privileges to all foreign traders and abolished the state's protective tariffs and monopolies. This resulted in a reversal of the import-export structure of the empire and led to the destruction of the textile industry in Ottoman Turkey. Soon many other branches of Ottoman industry became affected and by the late 1800s the whole of Ottoman industry was on the verge of collapse.[4] These developments thus marked the end of industrialization via the manufacturing sector and the empire was instead relegated to raw materials production geared to the needs of a world economy dominated by Europe; with its native industry destroyed, the Ottoman Empire gradually became transformed into an agrarian reserve of the expanding European capitalist economies.[5]

By the late nineteenth century, then, the Ottoman Empire had for all practical purposes become a semicolony of the expanding Western powers. Its economy was mortgaged to foreign capitalists and their states, widespread revolts and rebellions had occurred throughout its conquered territories, and new social groups had emerged that began posing problems for its continued, if ill-fated, existence under the rule of the sultans and the palace bureaucracy.

The Western powers, taking advantage of these problems, found their way in through direct economic controls and later through military occupation of large parts of Ottoman territory at the end of the nineteenth and beginning of the twentieth centuries—actions that culminated in the occupation of virtually every corner of the empire during World War I.[6]

Following the collapse of the Ottoman Empire at the end of the war, Britain, France, Italy, and other Western powers colonized its territories and remained in control of its various provinces for several decades. "The Ottoman military defeat by the British and French during the First World War," writes Roger Owen, "produced a radical change throughout the whole Middle East."

> [T]he Arab provinces of the empire were carved up into a number of successor states, each of them under the control of one or other of the victorious powers; the new Syria and Lebanon under the French; the new Iraq, Palestine and Trans-Jordan under the British.[7]

Thus, "by the mid-1920s," continues Owen, "the British and the French were the masters of the Middle East."

> It was they who determined almost all of the new boundaries; they who decided who should rule, and what form of governments should be established; and it was also they, in association with the Americans, who had a major say in how access to the region's natural resources should be allocated, particularly the oil fields.[8]

In sum, from the Persian Gulf to Palestine, down to the Suez Canal and the Arabian Peninsula, and across North Africa, much of the territories of the empire came under the jurisdiction of Britain, France, and other Western powers. These divided up these lands amongst themselves to secure trade routes, raw materials, and new markets for the expanding world economy controlled by Europe.

Historical Background

Ever since the decline and disintegration of the Ottoman Empire in the late nineteenth century, the Middle East has been at the center of struggles between the chief imperialist powers of the West, the object of which was control over the oil needed to fuel their expanding capitalist economies.[9] The history of the Middle East in the twentieth century, as Joe Stork has pointed out, is thus "linked to the efforts of the Western powers to secure absolute control over its resources and trade. The primary resource is oil. European (and later American) control of oil was achieved through a series of concessions to European companies."[10] As a result, "control of petroleum resources became the overriding focus of Western rivalry in the area and the main impetus for the Western powers to establish and maintain political and economic control over the region."[11]

Britain and France were the major forces behind the penetration of the Middle East until the end of the nineteenth century; but from that point on there emerged a renewed German interest in the region, resulting in a massive infusion of German capital.[12]

Referring to the intense rivalry between the chief European powers over control of the Middle East, Alain Gresh and Dominique Vidal write:

> What Paris, London, Berlin, and the others were after was raw materials at low prices, profitable investments for their capital, markets for their products, and the guarantee of safe lines of communication. Hence the influx of foreign capital. . . . Through this invasion, Europe controlled banking, the means of transport and communication (railways, ports, roads), the main services (water, gas, electricity, telephone), mining enterprises and, of course, oil.[13]

Edward Mead Earle, in his now-classic study *Turkey, the Great Powers, and the Bagdad Railway: A Study in Imperialism*, writes:

> Strategically, the region traversed by the Bagdad Railway is one of the most important in the world.
> Turkey-in-Asia, furthermore, was wealthy. It possessed vast resources of some of the most essential materials of modern industry: minerals, fuel, lubricants, abrasives. Its deposits of oil alone were enough to arouse the cupidity of the Great Powers. . . . It was anticipated that the Ottoman Empire would prove a valuable source of essential raw materials, a satisfactory market for finished products, and a rich field for the investment of capital. Economically, the territory served by the Bagdad Railway was one of the most important undeveloped regions of the world.[14]

During the course of the twentieth century, the major Western capitalist powers have engaged in rivalry over control of oil in the Middle East, a commodity that has proven to be vital for the industrial engines of the advanced capitalist states that have dominated the world economy. Over the past century, there have occurred three historic periods of interimperialist rivalry between the chief capitalist powers in the world economy: (1) the period from the final decade of the nineteenth century to World War I; (2) the interwar period, from 1918 to

1939; and (3) the postwar period, from 1945 to the Persian Gulf War of 1991. Each of these periods contains several phases, consisting of rivalry, dominance, challenge, and war. Interimperialist rivalries in all three periods have led to wars of redivision of the world and have established spheres of influence and control for the dominant forces that have emerged as victorious at the conclusion of these cycles of conflict and rivalry on a world scale. These cycles can be periodized, together with their various phases, as follows:

1. *The First Period:* the period from 1888 to 1914—from the height of British imperialism in the closing decades of the nineteenth century to the rivalry between the chief capitalist powers (Britain, France, Germany, and the United States) through the first decade of the twentieth century over the spoils of the collapsing Ottoman Empire, which led to the First World War.

2. *The Second Period:* the period from 1918 to 1939—the interwar years—during which the victorious powers (Britain and, to a lesser extent, France) exerted their control and influence over the world political economy and extended their imperial rule over vast territories across North Africa and the Middle East down to the Persian Gulf and the Arabian Peninsula. This period of British and French domination gave rise to the German and Japanese challenge and ultimately led to the Second World War.

3. *The Third Period:* the period from 1945 to 1991—the postwar period—during which the United States emerged as the sole capitalist superpower. It dominated the economies of its main twentieth-century capitalist rivals, as well as much of the rest of the capitalist world, thus giving it an unprecedented position in the world political economy. It controlled a substantial portion of the world's resources and wealth through neocolonial domination.

In the period since the Persian Gulf War of 1991, the United States has become the sole arbiter of crises and conflicts in the Middle East. With the collapse of the former Soviet Union and its previous influence in Middle East affairs, the U.S. role in this region has vastly increased.

To better understand the impact of Western imperialism on the Middle East during the past century, let us take a closer look at the dynamics and contradictions of each of these periods within the context of the social and political transformations that have been taking place in this region up to the present.

The First Period: 1888 to 1914

The first period of interimperialist rivalry between the major capitalist powers of the world—the period from the end of the nineteenth century to the First World War—witnessed the entry of the Western capitalist powers into the Middle East and the plunder of the Ottoman Empire.

Referring to "an epoch of three decades," covering the period from 1888 to 1918, "the history of those three decades," writes E. M. Earle, "is concerned largely with the struggles of European capitalists to acquire profitable concessions in Asiatic Turkey and of European diplomatists to control the finances, the vital routes of communication, and even the administrative powers of the Ottoman Government."[15]

> The coincidence between the economic motives of the investors and the political and strategical motives of the statesmen made Turkey one of the world's foremost areas of imperial friction. Its territories and its natural wealth were "stakes of diplomacy" for which cabinets maneuvered on the diplomatic checkerboard and for which the flower of the world's manhood fought on the sands of Mesopotamia.[16]

Earle goes on to point out that "oil exists in large quantities in Mesopotamia," and according to a 1901 report by a German technical commission on Mesopotamian petroleum resources, the region is characterized as "a veritable 'lake of petroleum' of almost inexhaustible supply."[17]

In 1904 the *Deutsche Bank,* of Berlin, promoters of the Bagdad Railway, obtained the privilege of making a thorough survey of the oilfields of the Tigris and Euphrates valleys, with the option within one year of entering into a contract with the Ottoman Government for their exploitation. Shortly thereafter Rear Admiral Colby M. Chester, of the United States Navy, became interested in the development of the oil industry in Asiatic Turkey. . . .

Here in the Near East, then, was a great empire awaiting exploitation by Western capital and Western technical skill.[18]

"The construction of the Anatolian Railways by German capitalists," Earle continues, "was accompanied by a considerable expansion of German economic interests in the Near East."[19] He writes: "That German traders should follow German financiers into the Ottoman Empire was to be expected. The *Deutsche Bank*—sponsor of the Anatolian Railways—had been notably active in the promotion of German foreign commerce. . . ."[20] Thus, through a variety of business ventures and government contracts German capital came to acquire a prominent economic position in the Ottoman Empire by the turn of the century:

Promoters, bankers, traders, engineers, munitions manufacturers, ship-owners, and railway builders all were playing their parts in laying a substantial foundation for a further expansion of German economic interests in the Ottoman Empire.[21]

The grand prize for German imperialism in the Middle East, however, was not the Baghdad Railway and the concessions associated with it, per se; nor was it the enormous commercial and banking operations that resulted from railway construction. The Baghdad Railway was the vehicle that would facilitate German access to and exploitation of the vast *oil fields* in the Mesopotamian valley, from Mosul to Baghdad to the Gulf, the territory where Iraq is located today.

As the rivalry between the major imperialist powers played itself out in the final phase of the Ottoman collapse during World War I, and as the terms of the Treaty of Versailles forced the liquidation of private foreign investments, including the Baghdad Railway, German influence in the Middle East virtually came to an end. While the French and the British struggled for some time to profit from the spoils of the Ottoman Empire and took most of its territories and turned them into French and British mandates, the United States began to take an active role in the commercial and financial activities of the Middle East, especially in the extraction of oil.

The Chester concessions played an important role in the expansion of U.S. business interests in the Middle East. The American promoters of the Chester railway lines were "granted exclusive rights to the exploitation of all mineral resources, including oil, lying within a zone of twenty kilometers on each side of the railway lines."[22] Moreover, the oil fields of Eastern Anatolia were projected to "provide rich sources of supply of raw materials" and it was projected that "in the construction of railways, ports, and pipelines there [would] be a considerable demand for American steel products."[23] Thus, Earle pointed out in the early 1920s:

> Economic development of the vast region through which the new railways will pass, promises to furnish a market for American products, such as agricultural machinery, and to offer ample opportunity for the profitable investment of American capital. The Chester project may well become an imperial enterprise of the first rank.[24]

Countering this American challenge to European control and dominance of the Middle East, Britain and France reemerged as the dominant powers. They consolidated their control of the region, overrunning the German presence there and keeping in check the U.S. challenge to British dominance, a situation that set the parameters of interimperialist rivalries in the Middle East in the second period.

The Second Period: 1918 to 1939

The second period of interimperialist rivalry between the chief capitalist powers of the world—the period generally identified as the interwar years—ushered in an era of outright colonization and partition of the Middle East, from the Persian Gulf to the shores of the Eastern Mediterranean.

> From its position of strength, the British Empire was able to grab the largest slice of the Ottoman cake, after the defeat of the Turks and their German allies. In accordance with the Sykes-Picot Agreement, the territories allocated after World War I to British administration, either directly or indirectly, comprised both what is nowadays called Iran, Iraq, and Jordan, the ports of Haifa and Acre in Palestine as well as a mandate for the latter, to which must be added England's possessions in Egypt, Sudan, the Arabian Peninsula and the Gulf.[25]

Thus, by the end of World War I, "Britain had secured a military hold over many of the Arab territories formerly under Ottoman rule, including Mesopotamia. . . . The division of the Arab territories between Britain and France following World War I . . . was certainly one of the more notorious exercises of imperialist power . . . [with] oil interests determining the final lines of the map of the Middle East."[26]

Britain, together with France as its junior partner, hence effectively established its dominance over large territories of the Ottoman Empire and secured direct access to sources of oil, thus controlling the lifeline of the industrial machine of Western Europe and many countries around the world.[27] With direct mandate over the land, resources, and people of the Middle East, British imperialism secured its leading position in this part of the world as the sole and undisputed capitalist superpower for nearly two decades.

> In October 1918 Great Britain struck the final blows in a brilliant campaign through which she gained mastery of the Arab

world. The Ottoman Empire was no more: Syria, Palestine, Trans-Jordan, and Iraq—all were under British control. Iraq was the greatest prize, perhaps the richest of the war, for within it were vast, untapped reserves of oil.[28]

In exerting its supremacy over the Middle East and other regions of the world, however, Britain came face-to-face with a new challenge to its rule, first by Germany through massive military action that led to World War II, and then by the United States by the war's end. Defeating its German rival at the conclusion of the war, the United States came to replace Britain as the world's leading capitalist superpower, defining the nature and dynamics of the global political economy in the third period.

The Third Period: 1945 to 1991

The third period of interimperialist rivalry extends from the end of World War II to the Persian Gulf War of 1991—the era generally referred to as the postwar period. In this third phase of global rivalry, the United States emerged as the leading Western power. It extended its control and influence not only over Europe and the Pacific basin, but also over the Middle East and the Persian Gulf.

In the decade following the end of World War II, the United States came to secure a dominant position in the Middle East. Its vigorous entry into the region "would bring to an end . . . more than a century and a half of [British] predominance in the Near and Middle East. . . . London would have to bear the cost of competition, not from France who was also being ousted from the region, but from the United States; the latter's rise in power would be in inverse proportion to Britain's decline."[29]

With the transfer into U.S. hands of ex-British mandates and spheres of influence from Palestine to Iran down to the Arabian Peninsula, the United States made inroads into the oil fields of the Middle East and the Gulf region, setting up a series of surrogate pro-U.S. neocolonial states stretching from Turkey and Israel to Iran and Saudi Arabia. With firm grip over such key client states in the region, the United States assured its geopolitical control over the region, securing its access to and exploitation of the vast oil resources of the Middle East and thus controlling a strategic commodity that is vital to the industrial engine of the advanced capitalist economies.[30]

During the 1950s, the United States extended its control over the entire Middle East region through: (1) the Truman Doctrine, which tied Greece and Turkey to U.S. interests; (2) links with the newly formed state of Israel as a U.S. outpost; (3) the transfer of control over the oil fields from British to American oil companies in Saudi Arabia; and (4) the CIA-engineered overthrow of the Mossadeq regime in Iran and the installation to power of the shah as a U.S. puppet to oversee the flow of oil in the Persian Gulf.

During the period from the early 1950s to the late 1970s the United States exerted its postwar dominance in the Middle East through massive arms transfers and military aid to Turkey, Israel, Saudi Arabia, and Iran to counter both the Soviet Union and, more importantly, its chief capitalist rivals—Britain, France, Germany, and Japan.

Interimperialist rivalries, which became visible in flows of import-export trade beginning in the mid-1970s, were played out between the chief capitalist powers vis-à-vis the two competing centers of regional power in the Middle East (Iran and Iraq) that controlled important sources of oil vital for the economies of the advanced capitalist countries.[31]

U.S. postwar dominance in the Middle East came under increasing pressure with the downfall of the Shah in Iran and the rise of Islamic fundamentalism throughout the region in the late 1970s and throughout the 1980s.[32] While persistent hostilities between Iran and Iraq led to the first Gulf War of 1980—a war fought for nearly a decade to settle the question of regional power in the Middle East—it also led to the regional realignment of rival imperialist powers engaged in the struggle for control of Middle East oil that culminated in the Persian Gulf War of 1991. The massive U.S. military intervention in Saudi Arabia and the subsequent invasion of Iraq reduced Iraq's military power in the region and acted as a check to the United

States' chief capitalist rivals, who had enlisted Iraq to look after their own economic interests in the Middle East.

The Post-1991 "New World Order" and its
Impact on the Middle East

In the aftermath of the defeat of Iraq in the Persian Gulf War of 1991, and following the collapse of the Soviet Union in the early 1990s, the United States declared a "New World Order" in which U.S. supremacy in the Middle East would be recognized by all parties. "This was the first war," write Haim Bresheeth and Nira Yuval-Davis, "in which the U.S. not only played a self-appointed, newly outlined role, that of world policeman, but also charged the world community a fee for its services."[33] They go on to add:

> Its [United States'] manipulations of the Security Council, and its strident opposition to any peaceful means of resolving the conflict, may well be a sign of a new order of things. . . . If so, this sign carries with it a sobering message to the under-developed, starving, indebted populations of the South, a message of additional hardship, strife and hunger in a unipolar world control system.[34]

With Soviet power swept away, and rival forces kept in check, the U.S. found its newly acquired monopoly of force convenient enough to redraw the boundaries of Great Power politics in the Middle East—one that has brought to the region a climate of tension and uncertainty.

During the 1990s, the U.S. role in the region became more fluid as the Arab-Israeli conflict became intensified through the rise of Islamic fundamentalism in the Occupied Territories. The eventual limited transfer of these territories to the Palestinians over the course of the decade did not result in the expected peace, as the political turmoil inherited from the late 1980s uprising (Intifada) in Gaza and the West Bank, continued Israeli repression, and U.S. imperialist encroachments further fanned the flames of discontent. Thus, the "New World Order" became a code word for a new form of imperialist control and domination of the Middle East under the aegis of the United States as the chief imperialist power of the late twentieth century.[35]

The increase in hostilities in southern Lebanon, the continuing political crisis in Cyprus, and the ongoing unrest in Gaza and the West Bank resulting from the construction of new settlements in East Jerusalem, as well as a political situation involving unsolved power struggles that are both internal and external to the region, have once again placed the Middle East in the forefront of conflict and political turmoil, and have produced more bloodshed and death in the most recent period.

The latest Israeli invasion of southern Lebanon and the indiscriminate killing of civilians in that country have raised new questions on the nature and role of U.S. imperialism, which has used right-wing allies as a regional police force to control and dominate the Middle East at the end of the twentieth century.

2

Nationalism, Ethnic Conflict, and Political Turmoil in the Middle East in the Early-Twentieth Century

The decline and fall of the Ottoman Empire at the beginning of the twentieth century had a profound effect on the people of Ottoman Turkey, especially on the minority ethnic groups (Greeks, Jews, and Armenians) that had secured an important position in the social, political, and economic institutions of Ottoman society. Among these groups, the most prominent were the Armenians.

The decline of the Ottoman Empire, in which Western imperialism played a key role, gave rise to an ultraconservative political reaction—one that singled out the Armenians as a scapegoat for the ills of Ottoman society. In a few short years of war and political turmoil across the empire, more than 1.5 million Armenians lost their lives in the planned pogroms, forced marches, and deportations in 1915.

This chapter examines the rise of nationalism, ethnic conflict, and political turmoil in the Middle East, with focus on the Armenian community in Ottoman Turkey in the early twentieth century.[1] It shows that the rise of Turkish nationalism was a reaction to Western imperialism (which precipitated the decline and fall of the Ottoman Empire), and that the subsequent hostilities directed toward ethnic minorities, particularly the Armenians, led to the first mass genocide of the twentieth century.

The Role of Ethnic Minorities in Ottoman Society

Ethnic minorities, made up of Armenians, Greeks, Jews, and numerous other national groups situated throughout the Ottoman Empire, played an important role in the Ottoman social structure. Concentrated mainly in Istanbul and Izmir, the Greeks, the Armenians, and, to a lesser extent, the Jews had already obtained a commanding lead in Ottoman trade and finance by the late eighteenth century.[2] As the ethnic population grew in size over the decades, their position further improved and began to play a dominant role in key branches of the Ottoman economy by the end of the nineteenth century. In the Ottoman capital, Istanbul, Armenians, Greeks, and Jews together constituted upwards of half the population of the city during this period. Of the 1 million inhabitants of Istanbul, 500,000 were Turks, 400,000 were Armenians and Greeks, and 100,000 were Jews and Europeans.[3] Elsewhere, in Izmir and other major cities of the empire, although relatively smaller in population size the minority communities had obtained a disproportionate control of the local economy and reaped substantial wealth from the empire's commerce, finance, and other economic activities. A German account of the role of Greeks, Armenians, and Jews in the Ottoman economy, published in 1912 in Berlin, states:

> They have divided everything between them or together dominate the terrain. Practically all that concerns the immediate necessities of life is in Greek hands. All branches related less directly to living but rather to the acquisition of civilization are almost exclusively in the sphere of the Armenians; they have the large textile businesses, the large iron, tin, and zinc businesses, and also all that pertains to the building trade. Only the small fancy-goods, haberdashery, and colonial goods trades are left to the Jews. Even the money business—from large bankers down to paltry money-changers—is, in Constantinople, mainly in Greco-Armenian hands; there are only small Jewish bankers there, and very few money-changers. . . . The antiquity dealers and rug merchants of Constantinople are almost without exception Sephardim.[4]

In Izmir and Salonika, however, the Jews played a more active role in trade and commerce, though Greek and Armenian presence in the former was quite substantial.

In his book *The Economic History of the Middle East and North Africa*, Charles Issawi points out the central role played by Armenian, Greek, and Jewish merchants in the empire's import-export trade by focusing on "the growth of export-import firms that could handle and finance the outward flow of agricultural produce and the inward flow of manufactures and other consumer goods."[5] "These firms," he adds, "were almost wholly foreign."

> British in Egypt and Iraq, French in Syria and North Africa, British and Russian in Iran, British, French, Austrian, Italian, and others in Turkey. . . . Their access to the farmers was through small merchants and moneylenders recruited chiefly from minority groups—Armenians, Greeks, Jews, Syro-Lebanese Christians—who advanced money, bought crops for resale to the exporters, and marketed the goods consumed in the countryside. Sometimes minority members established their own contacts with Britain, France, and other industrial countries, setting up branches of export firms.[6]

"In Turkey," writes Issawi, "the Greeks, Armenians, and Jews, in that order, dominated the urban sector and controlled a considerable part of the rural."

> The Galata bankers, consisting of Levantines and minority members, had controlled finance, and their replacement by modern banks only enlarged the field; in 1912, of the 112 bankers and bank managers in the Ottoman Empire only one was a Muslim Turk. In industry, it has been estimated that only 15 percent of capital belonged to Turks. In commerce, Armenians and Greeks established themselves in Europe early in the 19th century and handled most of its trade with Turkey. In agriculture, *millets* were particularly active in such important cash crops as silk and cotton.[7]

A Turkish account of the economic activities of Greeks, Armenians, and Jews in western Turkey (mainly Istanbul and

Izmir) provides a more detailed description of their involvement in foreign export trade—in this case the shipment abroad of agricultural products:

> Almost all the produce from a vast segment of Anatolia connected with Izmir used to come there and fill the large area from the Fruit Market as far as the Customs. And in this area swarmed people of all nations and also those whose origins were unknown but who used to be known as the residents of Izmir. These people carried various papers of identification, as if they were Europeans, but their hive consisted of Greeks, Armenians, and especially Jews. This hive had a ceaseless activity, its members buzzing around and endlessly sucking the available honey supply to the extent of flooding their gizzards. There were also a few Turkish shops here and there. . . .
>
> When the producer in Anatolia was not bound by contract to a foreign export merchant, he would bring the remainder of his crop to the middlemen at the Fruit Market. . . . Thus, the Turkish merchants constituted mostly, in fact wholly, this class of people who satisfied themselves by being the middlemen between the producers and the export merchants. . . .
>
> In this commercial battleground, the producers were the victims; the foreign and semi-foreign elements the profiteers; the Turks the onlookers. Certainly, the strongest, most active, and cleverest were the Jews.[8]

As this Turkish account of the role of ethnic minorities in the Ottoman formation clearly demonstrates, the Armenian, Greek, and Jewish tripartite ethnic enclave in Ottoman Turkey came to be viewed in Turkish eyes as a "semi-foreign element," having interests contrary to that of the vast majority of the Ottoman population and the Turkish nation in general. Strong, ideologically ridden nationalist views similar to the one expressed above were used by the Young Turks to fuel feelings of resentment among the Turkish population against all non-Muslim ethnic minorities in Ottoman society—especially against Armenians, with their close proximity to centers of Ottoman state power during the late nineteenth and early twentieth centuries.

The Position of the Armenian Community
in Ottoman Turkey

The number of Armenians in the Ottoman Empire during this period has been estimated at about 2.5 million, with over 80 percent living in rural areas, mainly in eastern Anatolia and in the Adana and Maras regions in the south.[9] In the main urban center, Istanbul, Armenians numbered some two hundred thousand at the beginning of this century. Izmir on the west coast; Erzurum, Kars, and Van in the east; Sivas and Amasya in the north-central region; and Adana, Mersin, Diyarbakir, and Maras in the southeast were other, less populated urban centers of Anatolia where Armenians were concentrated; they ranged from ten thousand to one hundred thousand in each of these medium-sized cities, with many more residing within each of the *vilayets*, or provinces.[10] The remainder of the Armenian population lived in small towns and villages throughout eastern and southern Anatolia, where they made a living by tilling their small plots of land. Only a small percentage of the Armenian population was made up of large landowners, while the vast majority was made up of peasants cultivating their own few acres of land.[11]

In the cities and urban centers, such as Istanbul and its adjacent municipalities, a different class structure prevailed: here, merchants, bankers, manufacturers, and middlemen played an important role, despite the fact that most Armenian city dwellers were either small business owners, craftsmen, or common laborers.[12]

According to the system of *millets* (national/ethnic communities) set up by Sultan Mohammed II in the fifteenth century, the Armenian Patriarch of Constantinople was designated as the leader of the *Ermeni millet*.[13] Under this system of political administration, the Patriarch was in charge of the religious, educational, and social life of the Armenians of the Ottoman Empire. However, "By the nineteenth century," writes Louise Nalbandian, "this Patriarchal office had become so weakened that the real power was not in the hands of the Patriarch but was held by an oligarchy comprised of wealthy conservative elements among the Armenians of Constantinople."[14]

> This oligarchy was drawn from the *amira* class, which consisted of bankers, rich merchants, and government officials. By controlling the Patriarch, the *amiras* dominated the national and much of the religious activity of the Armenians of Constantinople.[15]

Thus, by the early nineteenth century, the Armenian elite played a dominant role within the Armenian community, and was very influential in the Ottoman power structure as well, due in large part to their strategic position within the economy and state administration.

The bankers, constituting the dominant element of this elite, played a direct role in the empire's economy: they collected taxes, made loans to the state, insured funds against losses, and dominated foreign exchange and commercial operations, which brought them into close contact with Europe and the West.[16] As one close observer of Ottoman society notes:

> The magnates, known as *amiras*, played a dominant role in the Armenian church and community and an important one in Ottoman administration. One group of *amiras* consisted of *sarrafs*, or bankers, who furnished tax farmers and other provincial officials with the capital required for bidding and guaranteed that the stipulated tax revenues would be paid into the imperial treasury. By the beginning of the nineteenth century, Armenian bankers were prominent in foreign exchange and commercial operations as well.[17]

Thus, while the bulk of the Armenian urban population consisted of common laborers and craftsmen organized in guilds, or *esnaf*, the elite elements (led by the *amiras*) were clearly a dominant force in influencing the key institutions of Ottoman society as well as controlling the Armenian community itself.[18] As Adjarian explains:

> The *amiras* were the old Armenian government functionaries. Their emergence took place in the following manner. The government would nominate a Turkish Pasha as a governor,

the latter would designate an Armenian money-changer as guarantor for the payment of taxes; the money-changer would defray the expenses of the Palace and, after entering these against payable taxes, he would personally collect the taxes from the people. The *amiras* were mostly from the provinces and, as the most influential people in the country, would participate in all national (i.e., Armenian) affairs. The patriarch and the National Assembly were in their hands.[19]

Another group of Armenian magnates consisted of high government officials in charge of various state institutions or departments, including the imperial palace, the educational system, health, public works, and foreign affairs.[20] In addition, "The ministry of the Imperial Private Treasury [the sultan's personal wealth] was always in the hands of the Armenians."[21]

The pivotal position of this select segment of the Armenian population in the Ottoman state, economy, and society brought them to centers of power and influence within the Ottoman Empire well into the nineteenth century.

Ethnic Rivalry and the Rise of Turkish Nationalism

The expansion of the economic power of ethnic minorities (particularly Armenians) during the nineteenth century began to be felt by the Turkish population in both urban and rural areas, as the non-Moslem ethnic groups (Greeks, Armenians, and Jews) began to dominate the commercial and financial activities of the empire and bought up much of the arable land in the rural areas, while outcompeting their Turkish business rivals in the cities and towns where Turks had been the dominant force.[22] As wealth was transferred from Turkish to Armenian or Greek hands, and to a lesser extent Jewish ones, the widening gap between the Turks and these minority ethnic groups led to resentment against the prosperous sectors of the non-Muslim population who increasingly occupied center stage in the economy and society. As a trade report on the situation in Erzurum, in eastern Turkey, states:

An unequivocal sign of rising prosperity is to be found in the enhanced value of land. Within a short time it has doubled in price. This may be accounted for chiefly by the fairer treatment the cultivators experience under the Tanzimat. . . . It is, however, remarkable that the purchasers of land are universally Armenians, and the sellers almost always Mussulmans, a fact of strong significance as to the effect of the Tanzimat on the Christian part of the population, which is evidently rising in prosperity.[23]

Elsewhere in eastern Turkey,

Armenians occupied key positions in trade and business, which facilitated anti-Armenian agitation among the . . . Muslim masses, and in the first place the Kurds. For example, in the *vilayet* [province] of Sivas (where Armenians formed 35 percent of the population), out of 166 large importers 125 were Armenians; out of 37 bankers 32 were Armenians, and out of 9,800 small traders 6,800 were Armenians. Armenians owned 130 of the 150 industrial enterprises. In the *vilayet* of Van, Armenians held 98 percent of the trade, 80 percent of the agriculture. . . . There were 18 large merchants, all Armenian, 50 money-lenders (30 Armenians and 20 Turks), 20 money-changers, all Armenians, 1,100 craftsmen (1,020 Armenians and 80 Turks), 50 *rentiers* (20 Armenians and 30 Turks), 80 vegetable merchants (50 Armenians and 30 Turks), 200 fruit merchants, all Armenians. All members of the liberal professions—physicians, pharmacists, lawyers, etc.—were Armenians.[24]

In the western region of the empire—in Izmir, Bursa, and elsewhere—the situation was similar. According to a report by the British Foreign Office,

In Izmir the general improvement "however is more generally to the advantage of the Christian races who are . . . buying up the Turks." . . . The Turks, handicapped by conscription, "fall into the hands of some Christian usurious banker [Armenian, Greek, or occasionally European] to whom the whole property or estate is soon sacrificed. . . . [I]n the immediate vicinity of Smyrna very few Turkish landed proprietors remain."[25]

Further west, "Every one who has any familiarity with the Aeolic and Ionian coasts," reports British author W. M. Ramsay, "knows of many a flourishing Greek village, which not so many years ago was empty or peopled only by Turks. The Turks are losing, or have in places lost, their hold on the coast and on the valleys that open on the coast. . . . As the railway goes inland, the Greek element goes with it and even in front of it."[26]

"This feeling of being overwhelmed and driven out caused much resentment among Turks," writes Issawi, "and helps to account for the intense bitterness and violence in the struggle between Turks, Armenians, and Greeks in the period from 1895 to 1923."[27]

The prominence of the Armenian *amiras* within Ottoman society led to much bitterness among broad segments of the Turkish population, especially the nationalist elements within it, based primarily among the nationalist intelligentsia and generals and officers in the military. Such bitterness against wealthy Armenians soon turned into a generalized resentment against the Armenian community as a whole and gave rise to the brutal repression of Armenians and the massacres of 1894–96.[28]

The periodic looting and destruction of Armenian neighborhoods, the killings of large numbers of Armenians in selective, orchestrated massacres sanctioned by the government,[29] and the absence of Western intervention to halt the atrocities committed against the Armenian population set the stage for full-scale repression of the Armenian community with the rise to power of the Young Turk fascists led by Enver, Cemal, and Talat Pashas in the first decade of the twentieth century, and thus cleared the way for the "final solution" to "the Armenian question"—the extermination of 1.5 million Armenians in 1915.[30]

Ultranationalism and the 1915 Genocide of Armenians in Ottoman Turkey

Although numerous attempts in bringing about an Armenian national uprising in the east led to severe repression and massacres of thousands of Armenians at the end of the nineteenth century,[31] the turning point for the very survival of the Armenian community in Ottoman Turkey was the Young Turk revolution of 1908. "From the revolution's beginning," writes Paul Saba, "oppressed nations within the empire seized the occasion to declare their independence, while foreign powers sought to take advantage of Turkish internal disorder for their own gain."

> In 1908, Bulgaria announced its independence; soon after Crete revolted to unite with Greece. Austro-Hungary annexed Bosnia-Herzegovina and in 1911-12, Italy invaded and conquered Libya. Finally, in 1913, a united Balkan alliance drove the Turks out of Macedonia. Within the remnants of the Empire other oppressed nationalities, including the Armenians and the Arab peoples, were demanding greater autonomy or self-determination.[32]

It was within this context of disintegration of the Ottoman Empire and the attempt of the Turkish nationalist forces to salvage the pieces of the crumbling empire that the Young Turk reaction took its most ruthless form:

> Turkey jolted toward military dictatorship, and Turkification became the dominant ideology in leading CUP [the Committee of Union and Progress] and government circles. Pan-Turkism, as theorized by the CUP, was an extreme expression of the contradictory and ambivalent response of Turkish nationalists to Western penetration and its destructive impact on the unity of the Ottoman Empire. . . . Racialism, chauvinism, militarism, and a disregard for much of traditional Islam were all features of Pan-Turkism. Taken together, this combination of ideological elements foreshadowed a similar ideology which was to emerge in Germany in the 1920s: Nazism.[33]

"Pan-Turkish theorists," Saba points out, "conceptualized Turks as a master race, and envisioned the forcible creation of a great empire ('Turan') of all 'Turo-Aryan' peoples throughout Asia. Russia, the Slavic peoples, and Armenians were all seen as obstacles to this goal."[34]

The Turks were to be united in a new purified state in which there would be no place for "alien" peoples. The CUP's efforts at popular mobilization of the Turkish masses on the basis of nationalist appeals, racial intolerance and Nazi-like cults of the Turk's pagan past created a climate of growing intolerance for all minority peoples within the Empire.[35]

Within this context of the ideology of Pan-Turkish nationalist expansionism to the east, the Ottoman Empire entered World War I and hoped to overrun Russia as part of its strategy to reconquer ancient Turan. "Within two weeks of the campaign, however, 80 percent of the troops [of the Third Army] had been killed either by Russian forces or by the terrible Caucasian winter."[36]

Defeated in battle, the Young Turks determined to strike at an easier target. In early February 1915, the Central Council of the Committee of Union and Progress decided upon the systematic extermination of all Armenians within the Ottoman Empire. Armenian sympathy for Russia and their illegal possession of arms provided the pretexts, while the absence of allied observers in the area as a result of the war provided the opportunity for Turkish reaction to strike its blow virtually unobserved.[37]

Saba continues:

Planned, supervised and directed at every level by the Committee of Union and Progress with a fierce bland of racial fanaticism and 20th century rationalism, unrestrained by remorse or conscience, the same pattern of extermination was employed throughout the Armenian provinces. It was a pattern which, in many respects, foreshadowed the holocaust visited upon European Jewry by the Nazis.[38]

Thus the first genocide of the twentieth century unfolded in full force and continued until it consumed the lives of 1.5 million Armenians. It involved the rape, assault, plunder, and murder of an entire population with the premeditated, ultra-nationalist objective of wiping out the Armenian community of Ottoman Turkey.[39]

This act of planned genocide perpetrated against the Armenian people nearly achieved its stated aims, as most of the estimated 1.8 to 2 million Armenian inhabitants of Ottoman Turkey were exterminated through mass murder or marched to their deaths in the Syrian desert and the eastern plains. Less than 15 percent of the prewar Armenian population was able to escape the horror of the genocide and take refuge in Russia or other surrounding states; after the final collapse of the Ottoman Empire and the emergence of the new Turkish state in 1923, there were less than one hundred thousand Armenians remaining in the entire country.[40]

Some Concluding Observations

The Young Turk government's ultranationalist projection of power, extending to territories beyond that controlled by the Ottoman central state, was an attempt to establish a greater Turkish empire that reclaimed its historic central Asian heritage. The question of pan-Turkic expansionism to the east, then, must be seen in this context of the nationalist project, where ethnic conflict and rivalries were promoted to achieve imperial ends. It is, therefore, entirely logical to view the hostilities generated between Armenians and Kurds in eastern Turkey as part of the Young Turk campaign to suppress ethnic rebellions by way of setting ethnic groups against each other and thereby to clear the way for further Turkish territorial expansion.

The Armenians became the first victims of this political design. Caught between global, regional, and national power politics and standing in the way of the drive to establish a greater central Asian Turkish Empire, the Armenians paid a heavy price in the form of mass deportations, massacres, and annihilation of nearly all of their people. It is clear that outside powers were heavily involved in the final phase of the collapse and disintegration of the Ottoman Empire, whose territories were later directly occupied by the Western imperialist states during World War I. The particular position of the Armenians in this power struggle, identified as friend or foe by one or another of the contending forces in this conflict, cost the Armenians 1.5 million lives.

The fact that some Armenians had been close to centers of Ottoman power did not help the Armenian case either, as the proximity of Armenians to sensitive government posts to which they had access, and which could be utilized in a national uprising of Armenians in the eastern provinces, may have been an additional contributing factor justifying, in Turkish minds, the move to crush the Armenians and thereby eliminating this threat against the Ottoman state.

The Greeks and especially the Jews, mainly residing in large urban centers like Istanbul and Izmir, did not have any territorial claims; nor were they seen as standing in the way of Turkish expansionist plans. Likewise, the Ottoman provinces in North Africa and the Arabian Peninsula did not interfere with the Young Turks' ultranationalist vision, as they were too far from centers of power and control in this period of Ottoman decline and decay. Hence these regions were easily acquired by the European powers and turned into outposts of Western imperialism— the spoils being divided between France and Britain, the two dominant world powers at the time. The Greek invasion of western Turkey and the subsequent defeat of Greece in bloody battles in Izmir and elsewhere along the western coast of Turkey did result in the deaths of a large number of Greeks in Turkey during the war. The existence of a Greek homeland, however, provided a way out of the situation. There were mass deportations of Greeks to Greece, thereby avoiding a large-scale massacre.

The Armenians were accorded no such protection from the advancing Ottoman forces, who, through direct government orders, moved in with full force to remove them from their historic homeland. The forced marches and wholesale massacre of entire villages of Armenians eliminated all who stood in the path of the Turkish national project.[41]

3
Imperialism and the Resurgence of Nationalism in the Middle East

Turkey and Egypt

The resurgence of nationalism in the Middle East during the twentieth century was a response to the dominant role of Western imperialism in the region from the mid-nineteenth to the early twentieth century. The decline and fall of the Ottoman Empire during this period of crisis in the Middle East allowed the intrusion of European and U.S. imperialism into the region and thus prompted an anti-imperialist, nationalist response in Turkey, Egypt, Iraq, Syria, and other regions of the Middle East.

In this chapter we examine the origins and development of nationalist movements in Turkey and Egypt, and in the next chapter in Syria and Iraq—the four most prominent cases of twentieth-century nationalist movements that have succeeded in taking state power in the Middle East.

Imperialism and the Rise of Nationalism in Turkey

The nationalist movement in Turkey and the origins of the modern Turkish state go back to the Young Turks, who took power on the eve of the collapse of the Ottoman Empire. The rise of Mustafa Kemal and the Kemalists to the leadership of the national movement, and later the emergence of the new Turkish republic, owes its birth to the 1908 uprising—a political rebellion carried out against a corrupt and decaying imperial state apparatus with the aim of political reform to save the state from total collapse and disintegration.[1]

In the early 1900s, a growing number of military students in Istanbul were discontent with the policies of the despotic Ottoman state. Nationalist ideas were put forth by numerous intellectuals and journalists. Abdul-Hamid II, the ruling sultan, tried to suppress the movement by arrests, forced exile, and executions, but without success. Secret societies were formed in army headquarters throughout the empire and in Paris, Geneva, and Cairo. The most effective of these was the Committee of Union and Progress (CUP), or the Young Turks.[2]

The Young Turks remained in control of the state apparatus until its final collapse at the end of the First World War. The ultranationalist and dictatorial rule of the Young Turks during their decade-long reign, coupled with the massive territorial losses following the two Balkan Wars (1912–13), the massacre of 1.5 million Armenians between 1915 and 1918, and the failure of the government to safeguard Turkey from the onslaught of imperialist occupation forces during World War I, led to the collapse of the Ottoman Empire at the conclusion of the war. Bernard Lewis describes the situation in the final years of the Ottoman Empire this way:

> At the end of 1918 it seemed that the Sick Man of Europe was about to die at last. Resentment against the dictatorship of the Young Turk leaders had been mounting for some time; the advance of the Allied armies lent it a force that could no longer be resisted. . . .
>
> After three days of preliminary negotiation, on 29 October a Turkish delegation led by the Minister of the Navy Rauf Bey went on board H.M.S. *Agamemnon*, at anchor off Mudros, in the island of Lemnos, and signed an armistice next day. The Young Turk pashas, Talat, Enver, and Cemal, fled across the Black Sea on a German gunboat. An Allied fleet of sixty ships sailed past the silent guns of the Dardanelles, and on 13 November anchored in the port of Istanbul.[3]

For all practical purposes, the reign of the centuries-old Ottoman Empire had come to an end. Its government in disarray, its economy in shambles, and its territorial integrity threatened, the empire thus succumbed to the power of the Allies and surrendered its once-mighty rule over a vast territory across the Middle East.

On 8 December 1918 the Allied powers set up a military administration in Istanbul, the Ottoman capital:

> Allied troops occupied various quarters of the city, strict Allied control was established over the port, tramways, defences, gendarmerie, and police. . . . The Arab provinces of the Empire were already in Allied possession, and had been promised independence. Allied forces now began to threaten even the Turkish provinces themselves. French troops advanced from Smyrna into Cilicia and the Adana district. British forces occupied the Dardanelles, Samsun, Ayntab, and other strategic points, as well as the whole length of the Anatolian railway. On 29 April 1919 Italian troops landed at Antalya, to take possession of some of the areas assigned to them by the secret wartime agreements of the Allies.[4]

"Among the new leaders in the capital," writes Lewis, "even the will to independent survival seemed to have failed and political discussion centered on the form which Turkish subjection was to take, and on the relative merits of an American or a British mandate."[5] "There was indeed little room for hope," Lewis continues.

> Exhausted by eight years of almost continuous warfare, the once great Ottoman Empire lay supine in defeat, its capital defeated, its leaders in flight. The country was shattered, impoverished, depopulated, and demoralized. The Turkish people, beaten and dispirited, seemed ready to accept almost anything that the victors chose to impose on them.[6]

"Almost, but not quite," adds Lewis, "for when, under cover of Allied warships, a Greek army landed at Izmir in May 1919, the smouldering anger of the Turks was at last kindled into an inextinguishable blaze."[7] The stage was thus set for the emergence of a national movement, led by Mustafa Kemal and the

Kemalists, in a last-ditch effort to save the remains of a vastly reduced Turkish empire now confined to its Anatolian core.

Under the prevailing conditions in Ottoman Turkey during this period of occupation, the Kemalists decided that imperialism had to be defeated on three tactical fronts: the imperialist occupation forces; the Ottoman palace bureaucracy; and the minority comprador bourgeoisie.[8] Given the heavy concentration of imperialist forces in the major urban areas, the Kemalists withdrew to the Turkish countryside to organize and wage the national struggle.[9]

The immediate task of the nationalist leadership was to put together fighting forces throughout Anatolia to wage a full-scale offensive against imperialism and its local class agents. While the big landowners and the clergy had collaborated with the palace and the imperialist occupation forces in their areas, the natural ally of the nationalists was deemed by the Kemalists to be the Anatolian peasantry. It was in this group of small-holding peasants in Central and Eastern Anatolia, who were heavily dependent on the landlords and the clergy, that the nationalist leadership found its mass base to defeat imperialism and suppress internal reaction cultivated by the state, the landlords, and the comprador bourgeoisie.[10] Kemal's tactical maneuver with the landlords and the clergy to engage the peasantry on the side of the nationalists against the main enemy paid off in the short run in securing a nationalist victory.

Through this victory, Kemal, who had been struggling for an independent power base for the state bureaucracy, rallied his supporters around a new political party—the People's Party—which he founded in December 1922. By October 1923, Turkey secured its independence and Kemal was elected the first president of the republic. This marked the beginning of the reign of the petty-bourgeois, nationalist bureaucratic elite and the movement toward the consolidation and institutionalization of bourgeois nationalism that was to open the way for independent, national-capitalist development in Turkey.[11]

The Kemalist "bourgeois revolution," writes Turgut Taylan, "gave birth to a strong and centralized state that actively interfered in every aspect of social life."

[I]t destroyed irreversibly the political, juridical and ideological bases of the old pre-capitalist state and laid the basis for
the construction of a new type of state—a bourgeois republic
that paved the way for the subsequent development of the
capitalist mode of production.[12]

The state's role in the economy began to expand in the 1920s
as it entered various branches of local industry to develop the
infrastructure, establish banks, and regulate commerce.[13] Among
the most notable activities of the state in the spheres of industrial
production and finance were the development and expansion
of state-owned and controlled enterprises and the establishment
of several major industrial and commercial banks. In addition,
the state acquired full ownership and control of the petroleum
industry, the railways, major seaport facilities, and a number of
enterprises in the mining industry.[14]

The Great Depression of 1929 had a major impact on the
Turkish economy, and this led the state to assume a more force-
ful role as entrepreneur during the 1930s, taking on may of the
tasks traditionally performed by the national industrial bourgeoisie.[15] With the increase in the number of public enterprises
from 470 in 1927 to 1,473 in 1933, the state came to play a
central role in the national economy at the end of the 1920s and
during the 1930s.[16] However, while the state-capitalist development of the 1930s significantly improved Turkey's overall
economic position and placed the country on a favorable footing
with respect to industrialization, it at the same time sharpened
the contradictions inherent in the system, as the accumulation
of capital under the state-capitalist regime in Turkey during this
period was mainly achieved through the intensified exploitation of wage labor in public as well as private industries.[17] In
this sense, the contradiction between state (and private) capital
and wage labor constituted the primary contradiction in Turkey
during this period.[18]

At the same time, several other contradictions internal to
the state-capitalist system contributed to increased conflict
between the state and various classes within the country, the most
decisive of which was that between the state and the landlords

and compradors allied with imperialism. The landlords blocked all attempts to redistribute land to small-holders and landless peasants, attempted to prevent the development of cooperatives, manipulated the programs intended to serve poor peasants by diverting public funds granted for local development projects into their own private accounts, and resisted capitalist development to preserve their oligarchic position in the countryside over the impoverished peasantry. The Turkish compradors likewise resisted all attempts by the state to transform them into industrial capitalists. Being accustomed to their position as middlemen between the landlords and imperialists involved in import-export trade and other commercial ventures, they viewed the policies of the state as a threat to their cozy relations with the landlords and the imperialists. Consequently, they boycotted all efforts at independent national capitalist development initiated by the state.[19]

This "natural" alliance of compradors and large landowners coincided with the interests of U.S. imperialism in the region. Taking advantage of the opening afforded by the postwar crisis of state capitalism in the latter half of the 1940s, the United States became more and more involved in propping up the landlord-comprador forces to help bring them to state power by the end of the decade. The late 1940s thus marked a new stage in Turkey's postwar political economy. This period witnessed the final and decisive phase of the struggle between the Kemalist state and the landlord-comprador interests, which, with increased financial and political support provided by the United States, managed to capture state power in 1950. The coming to power of the landlord-comprador forces, which set the country in a new course, secured the U.S. hold on Turkey and helped effect the consolidation of Turkey's place in the world capitalist economy.[20]

As Taylan points out, "[T]he new direction came in response to the changes that arose in the capitalist world economy in the immediate aftermath of the war ... [as well as] changes in the lineup of class forces inside Turkish society, changes which greatly facilitated the new turn."

Successive governments of the ruling RPP [Republican People's Party] had alienated the big landowners and the rural bourgeoisie through policies which, added to the effects of wartime hardships, greatly damaged the agricultural sector. The urban commercial bourgeoisie had also come into increasing conflict with the RPP since the inception of the so-called "statism." The clash over the Land Reform Act of 1945 . . . acted as the immediate background to a split within the RPP. The Democrat Party which was formed on the basis of this split soon came to represent an alliance of the rural bourgeoisie and big landowners with the urban commercial bourgeoisie. This alliance, feeding upon the discontent of the peasant masses and sections of the urban proletariat, would come to power in 1950 and rule the country for ten years.[21]

The Demokrat Parti rule during the 1950s brought a full-scale transformation of the national state-capitalist regime into a neocolonial appendage of imperialism dominated by the transnational monopolies. Discontent of the masses against government actions in both domestic and foreign policy led to mass protests and uprisings at the end of the 1950s that were brutally suppressed by the Menderes regime and led to the military coup of May 1960. Superficial reforms to calm an angry populace did not stop the masses from pressing forward with more radical demands during the 1960s and resulted in more repression. There was a turn to the extreme right through the military intervention of March 1971 and again in September 1980, when tens of thousands of workers, trade unionists, students, and progressive intellectuals, lawyers, and journalists were locked up in the prisons and concentration camps of the military regime. Many were to be tortured and die there.[22]

During the decade of the 1980s, Turkey experienced a more profound conservative trend emanating from the rise and spread of Islamic fundamentalism. Extending from the influence of the Islamic Revolution in Iran and reinforced by rightist forces interested in keeping a check on labor and other progressive movements threatening the regime during this period, the Islamic reaction came to serve an important role in maintaining social control while moving Turkish society in a more conservative direction. This proved to be the case well into the 1990s, when by the middle of the decade Islamic rule became institutionalized in Turkish politics. Notwithstanding the military's recent moves against the fundamentalist forces that led to the forced resignation of the head of state, Necmettin Erbakan, the strength of the Islamic forces has continued to pose a serious threat to secular politics in Turkey at the end of the 1990s.

The crisis of the neocolonial regime in Turkey reached new heights with the accession to power in 1999 of a new coalition government that includes the fascist Nationalist Action Party (NAP) as one of the power brokers. The combination of the externally oriented capitalist policies and the succession of right-wing reactionary regimes over the past two decades have intensified the contradictions of Turkish society at the end of the twentieth century.

Imperialism and the Resurgence of Nationalism in Egypt

With the collapse of the Ottoman Empire at the end of the First World War, Britain, France, and other European powers moved in and occupied the various provinces of the now defunct empire. Britain became the dominant occupying force throughout the Middle East, and remained in the region through the first half of the twentieth century. It was during this period of colonial rule that Britain set up a series of governments responsive to British interests in the region including Egypt, Palestine, Jordan, Iraq, Kuwait, and a chain of dependencies in the Persian Gulf.

While local rulers (sultans and governors) were retained as figureheads, these territories came to serve the economic and strategic interests of British imperialism. Access to oil and other raw materials was secured; passage to India, China, and other parts of the Far East and its trade routes was ensured; and there was military domination of a strategic region joining three continents, bringing the Eastern Mediterranean, Suez and the Gulf region under Western imperialist control. Egypt played an important role in all this by providing use of the Suez Canal, linking Europe and the Mediterranean with the Indian Ocean via the Red Sea.

> Middle Eastern oil was regarded as vitally important to Britain's economic and strategic interests at the end of the First World War because it was seen to have displaced coal as fuel. . . .
> The Suez Canal was central to the exploitation of Middle East oil; there was no other worthwhile route from Abadan to Britain, and oil became a major cargo on the northbound route. . . . Britain was the chief user of this oil, importing in the 1930s five times as much as the next largest customer.[23]

"The Suez Canal clearly played an important role in Britain's international position at the beginning of this century," writes Richard C. Whiting.

> While the Canal brought India closer to Britain, it also effected even greater savings in the journey from Bombay or Calcutta to European ports. . . . The greatly improved ability of the Indian economy to sell goods directly to Europe . . . allowed that country to consume British exports. . . . It was because Britain could meet her trading deficits with Europe by sending exports to India, purchases which were in turn financed by sales of primary commodities to industrial Europe, that Britain's international position remained viable. . . .[24]

Thus, "from its opening in 1869 until 1956 the Suez Canal was regarded as a key feature of the British economy"[25] and played a central role in Britain's dominant position in the Middle East, as it did in the expansion of its global empire. This, in turn, became a rallying point for Egyptians to free Egypt from the shackles of British imperialism.

Nationalist sentiment ran deep among the Egyptian intellectuals, youth, and junior officers in the army, who resented the imperialist occupation of their soil and the dictates of Britain and the European powers over the social, economic, and political life of their nation. Supported by a series of revolts of poor peasants and agricultural workers and by industrial workers' strikes in the late 1940s and early 1950s, the nationalist forces in the army led by Gamal Abdel Nasser orchestrated a successful coup in 1952 that overthrew the king and the monarchy that had been propped up by British imperialism.

"On the night of July 22, 1952," writes Kirk J. Beattie, "the Free Officers went into action to seize control of the military and topple the government."

> The takeover was nearly bloodless (less than ten were killed and not many more wounded). Yusuf Siddiq fortuitously mobilized his band of twelve officers and sixty to seventy infantrymen ahead of schedule. Assisted by Faruq al-Ansari (from the armored corps), he secured control of Army General Headquarters, arresting Chief of Staff Gen. Hussein Farid and many other senior staff officers. Control of various military camps and air bases followed, as did seizure of the major remaining target, the broadcast station. The Suez Canal road was secured to deter intervention by British forces.[26]

News of the coup was announced on the radio on the morning of 23 July. Within a few days, King Farouk was deposed and the coup leaders, in firm control of the centers of power, declared themselves as the new government:

> Early on the morning of July 26 tanks surrounded Ras el-Tin palace. Some of the Royal Guards resisted, and there was a skirmish resulting in seven wounded. By this time the King was afraid for his life and signed the act of abdication. . . . Theoretically, Egypt was to remain a monarchy for another eleven months, but in fact the century and a half of the Muhammad Ali dynasty had come to an end.[27]

The victory of the Free Officers in deposing the monarchy ushered in a period of state capitalism in the national economy.[28] As in the case of Turkey and other nationalist regimes, the Nasser regime rallied the support of broad segments of the masses and used the state as an instrument of national capitalist development under petty-bourgeois bureaucratic rule.

The petty-bourgeois class nature of the Egyptian state

under the Nasser regime set the framework for political action that the bureaucratic officialdom undertook during this period. True to its petty-bourgeois nationalist aspirations and plans of development through direct intervention in the national economy, the Nasser regime took upon itself to launch a comprehensive national economic program to build the basis of an integrated capitalist economy that would at the same time advance the class interests of the national and petty bourgeoisie.

During the initial, state-capitalist period the state took a number of specific measures to facilitate the development of the national economy. First, land reform laws were passed in late 1952 to eliminate semifeudal production relations in the countryside and to facilitate industrialization in the urban areas. Next, a series of articles in the 1956 constitution outlined the role private capital must play in serving the national economy within the framework of a state-directed national economic plan. Following this, the state embarked on a policy of nationalization of foreign firms, including banks, and began development of a capital-goods sector based on the expansion of the iron and steel industry.[29]

> The land reform law passed in September 1952 . . . was designed to liquidate a feudal system, put an end to the misery of millions of peasants, and ensure the economy moved towards further industrialization. . . .
> The 1956 constitution . . . stressed that private capital should be directed towards serving the national economy. . . .
> The nationalization of the Suez Canal and of British and French firms, and the Egyptianization of foreign banks . . . [were carried out to facilitate the state's mandate] that Egypt should manufacture its own capital goods. Thus, the iron and steel industry was at the top of the state's list of priorities.[30]

In response to the Anglo-French invasion of Egypt in the Suez War in 1956, the government confiscated all British and French property and launched a mass retaliatory policy of nationalization and Egyptianization of foreign capital through the passage of laws that would transfer foreign-owned businesses to Egyptian citizens, especially to the Egyptian government:

A series of laws issued in January 1957 obliged all foreign banks and insurance companies to Egyptianize themselves, and British and French banks, such as Barclay's and Credit Lyonnais, were sold to Egyptian banks. Together with the nationalization of the Suez Canal company, this meant that the greater part of the foreign share in the Egyptian economy had been liquidated. Much of this share was transferred to the Egyptian Government, and between 1957 and 1960 a number of public economic organizations were created, while others already in existence were expanded.[31]

This mass transfer of property to the state facilitated the growth and expansion of the state's share in the national economy and led to greater prominence of the public sector in economic affairs. It was during this period of heightened nationalist activity that Egypt entered into its short-lived union with Syria under the rubric of the United Arab Republic (an episode that will be discussed in the next chapter).

Reflecting its central position in the economy, the Egyptian state played an active role in initiating development projects through five-year plans. This was followed by a series of further nationalization of private firms in industry, finance, trade, and consumer goods. In this way, the state came to assume a major role in promoting and directing the national economy on behalf of private capital. Thus, the state became the key agent of capital accumulation and the main source of capitalist development that transformed Egypt into a developing capitalist state.[32]

The state's central role in the Egyptian economy continued through the 1960s, when the size of the public sector expanded and most industries came under the state's control. As large businesses were nationalized and brought under the jurisdiction of the state, private capital was restricted to small-scale commodity production and local trade within the framework of a competitive market. Small business thus became the model of national capitalism in the spheres of production and exchange that remained outside the boundaries of the state-capitalist economy.

Although the state succeeded in its economic goals of fostering national industrialization during the state-capitalist period, the narrow bureaucratic and technocratic perspective of state officials prevented them from developing a clear understanding of Egyptian society and its class divisions. Without a class perspective on the prevailing social structure, the new rulers ended up supporting and enhancing capitalist relations of production in a new state-sanctioned setting.[33] Thus, together with the nationalization of foreign firms, development of cooperatives, and promotion of government ownership of banks and production facilities that promoted national industrialization, this period also witnessed the gradual expansion of private capital that later came to challenge the very basis of the state-capitalist economy.

Following the death of Nasser in 1970, open conflict between the public and private sectors began to develop as the state-capitalist economy entered a period of severe crisis. From this point on, the private capitalist sector scored some big gains and challenged the economics of Nasserism from which it itself had emerged in an earlier period.[34]

"What were some of the real reasons for the economic policy shifts after Nasser's death?" asks Ahmad Azim. He provides us the following answer:

> First and foremost was the gradual (but continuous) collaboration of the traditional and new (state) bourgeoisie with US imperialism. Second, after Nasser's death in September 1970, two levels of struggle ensued: the power struggle among those who had been close to Nasser, and the class struggle among the competing groups. Third, Sadat, in his struggle for power, allied himself with right-wing elements that were waiting in the wings. Fourth, the active influence—primarily economic in nature—of conservative Arab regimes increased. Fifth, the active influence of Western powers, in particular the United States, became overwhelming. All these contributed to the transition to a new, "open door" economic policy called *infitah*.[35]

The objectives of *infitah*, Azim says, were threefold: "to attract foreign capital; to encourage the Egyptian private sector; and to alter the nature of the Egyptian public sector."

> The government stressed the advantages and benefits of
> foreign capital, and the powerful mainstream mass media
> campaigned vigorously in favour of inviting foreign capital.
> The real motive behind such pronouncements, however, was
> the plan to transform the economic structure in the direction
> of undermining and dismantling the public sector.[36]

The gradual integration of Egypt into the world capitalist economy during this period paved the way for the disintegration of state capitalism and the emergence of a new (formerly bureaucratic) national capitalist class allied with the largest commercial and landowning interests. Together they would lead a new coalition of dominant class forces dependent on imperialism.

The transition to a neocolonial dependent capitalist economy further enhanced the penetration of foreign capital into Egypt during the 1970s and 1980s and reversed the trends set into motion in the early 1950s through the 1960s. With the shift in the balance of forces in the world economy in the postwar period in favor of the United States, U.S. investment and interest in Egypt became more pronounced in the post-Nasser years. By the early 1980s total foreign and joint venture investments had reached $10 billion, and, except for the banking sector, the overwhelming majority of these investments had come from the United States.[37]

The development of neocolonialism in Egypt was the logical outcome of the evolution of state capitalism that promoted and supported local capital, which, under conditions of worldwide domination of imperialism, became inescapably subordinated to foreign capital in a new relationship that assured the former's limited survival. Thus, as in Turkey and elsewhere in the Third World, state capitalism in Egypt facilitated the transition to a neocolonial capitalism dependent on imperialism. Today, at the close of the twentieth century, the course of development followed in Egypt has led to increased divisions and conflict between the contending class forces in Egyptian society and has created an unstable situation with immense political implications for the entire Middle East.[38]

Conclusion

The rise of nationalism and nationalist movements in the Middle East that fought to gain independence from Western colonial and imperialist domination during the twentieth century led to the establishment of a variety of state-capitalist regimes in the region in the postwar period. The rising tide of national struggles during this period played an important role in resisting imperialist domination.

In time, these regimes grew and matured into fairly developed capitalist states in the latter half of the twentieth century. Such development on the capitalist path led to the emergence of new class forces that became instrumental in reintegrating these newly independent states into the world economy through renewed neocolonial alliances.

The experience of Turkey and Egypt on this nationalist, state-capitalist path shows that, despite their original anti-imperialist posture, capital accumulation in Third World countries remaining within the world economy controlled by the imperialist states inevitably leads to neocolonialism. The two radical-nationalist states that we have examined in this chapter illustrate the process of late-twentieth-century capitalist development that defines the parameters of the contemporary global political economy.

4

Imperialism and the Resurgence of Nationalism in the Middle East

Syria and Iraq

For four centuries, from the early sixteenth to the early twentieth, the region encompassing today's Syria and Iraq was part of the territory of the Ottoman Empire. With the collapse of the empire at the end of the First World War, Syria and Iraq, as well as the neighboring territories of Lebanon, Palestine, and Trans-Jordan, came under the control and jurisdiction of the two victorious imperialist superpowers, Britain and France.

In dividing up these territories between them, the British and the French laid claim to different regions of the empire, with France assuming the League of Nations mandate over Syria and Lebanon, and Britain over Iraq. Turning this region into a colonial outpost of the West, the British and French mandates over these territories lasted until the middle of the twentieth century.

This chapter examines the impact of imperialism and the origins and development of nationalism in Syria and Iraq. Responding to the colonial occupation of Arab lands throughout the region, the nationalist movements in these countries waged a protracted struggle to take state power and succeeded in their aim to establish independent nation-states in Syria and Iraq, respectively.

Imperialism and the Nationalist Response
in Syria

Once subjected to the tributary rule of the despotic Ottoman state, the peasants and small-scale commodity producers of Syria increasingly came under the control of big landowners, merchants, and capitalists who were kept in power by the colonial regime during the French mandate after the collapse of the Ottoman Empire at the end of the First World War. Semifeudal production relations flourished in the countryside, while capitalist relations were promoted in commerce and industry in the urban areas such as Damascus and Aleppo. Given its special geographic location, Beirut in neighboring Lebanon was turned into a regional commercial center that facilitated the penetration of French capital into Syria and the rest of the Middle East.[1]

"Syria was the last of a long line of territories to fall into the orbit of the French empire," writes Derek Hopwood.

> The French entered Syria as conquerors. . . . The High Commissioners held all the power and the first three were generals who had gained colonial experience in Africa. To run the administration behind a Syrian facade they appointed French officials and advisers. . . . [M]ilitary expenditure in Syria was ten times that on civilian projects and France had always to use military force (or the threat of it) to maintain its authority.[2]

Using an age-old colonial scheme to maintain control over its subject peoples, France resorted to the divide-and-rule policy of setting various religious and ethnic groups against each other to achieve its ends. "Under French Mandate," writes Nikolaos Van Dam, "sectarian loyalties were deliberately incited in order to prevent or suppress the rise of Arab nationalism."

> As part of a divide-and-rule policy, the French favoured the military recruitment of special detachments among Alawis, Druzes, Kurds, Circassians and other minorities, who then formed part of the *Troupes Speciales du Levant* used to maintain order and to suppress local rebellions. The fact that these troops were largely composed of minorities increased the resentment among the Arabic-speaking Sunnis. Discord between

and within religious and ethnic minorities was also provoked by the fact that the French played off one tribal leader against another.[3]

Despite these divisions fostered by French colonialism to maintain its tight grip over Syria, the response to repressive colonial rule over the territory took more and more a national character. Nationalism in Syria emerged as an increasingly secular mass ideology based on a unifying experience of struggle for national identity and national independence.

The French mandate over Syria lasted nearly three decades, during which there was constant struggle on the part of the Syrian nationalists to wrest political power from France. The national struggle in Syria developed throughout the course of the French Mandate, from 1920 to 1946. This period witnessed the Great Revolt of 1925 and the General Strike of 1936, as well as other protracted nationalist activity against the colonial regime. The national movement continued to press for Syrian independence and fought to the bitter end to force France to give up its prized colonial possession. Weakened by its defeat in World War II and faced with increasing protests and demonstrations in Damascus and other cities across Syria, France was no longer able to maintain its stronghold over this territory and was driven out of Syria by 1946, the year when Syria gained its independence.[4]

During the decade following independence, Syria went through a period of coups and countercoups—including three in 1949, one in 1951, and another in 1954—by rival political forces vying for state power through the instrumentality of the military to accomplish their aims.

The first coup in postindependence Syria following the war in Palestine established the central role of the Syrian military in political affairs, a feature of Syrian politics for decades to come. "Seething popular discontent, quarrels between generals and politicians over responsibility for the Palestine disaster, charges and counter-charges of corruption," writes Tabitha Petran, "created a state of near anarchy. On 29 March 1949, Colonel Za'im seized power, ousted and exiled President Quwatly, dissolved parliament, and established military rule."[5] "This first overturn in the Arab world after the Palestine war," Petran continues, "was engineered by the American embassy in Damascus."

> Revelations of the directing United States role made in 1969 by Miles Copeland, a member of the 1949 embassy team, confirmed long-held Syrian suspicions.
>
> To Washington, striving to develop a policy to block communism and challenge British supremacy in the Arab East, Arab armies (originally organized as internal police forces) appeared the most likely stabilizing influence in an area threatened by mass upheavals.[6]

The subsequent coups and countercoups pushed and pulled Syria in and out of various alliances, with greater or lesser U.S. influence exerted, depending on the regime in power:

> The first fruit of the new American policy was the Za'im coup [in March 1949]. After a brief flirtation with Iraq, Za'im cemented close relations with Egypt and Saudi Arabia. But he was shortly overthrown by Colonel Sami Hinnawi in an Iraqi-engineered coup in August, presumably supported by Britain. Hinnawi attempted to pull Syria into the Hashemi camp. In December, when union with Iraq seemed imminent, Hinnawi was ousted by Colonel Adib Shishakli who returned Syria to the Saudi-Egyptian orbit. And a measure of American influence was restored.[7]

The heightened political activity through the series of military coups that took place during the initial years of the post-independence period in Syria was a reflection of the class struggles that continued after the overthrow of the monarchy. The coups and countercoups of this period were the political manifestations of the struggles between various classes and class factions striving to capture state power, especially the struggle between different wings of the national and petty bourgeoisie. However, pressures from below—from popular forces mobilized by nationalist sentiment, as well as by class interest—played an equally powerful role in shaping events during this period.

"In 1950 and 1951," writes Petran, "the peasants' movement reached its height. Peasant unrest erupted in all parts of the country. Peasants refused to render feudal services and dues and effectively abolished these practices in most areas."[8]

> In the Ghab, when reclamation work started, peasants fought landlords who arrived to lay claim to the land. Landlords expelled peasants from their villages, killed their livestock, and harassed them in every possible way. But other villages gave ousted peasants refuge; peasants remained united and stood together against the landlords. In mid-September 1951, thousands of delegates from all over Syria thronged to a peasants' congress in Aleppo convened by Hourani's ASP (Arab Socialist Party). Here they raised the slogan "land to the peasants," demanded real agrarian reform and a law to regulate relations between landlords and peasants. The congress gave the peasant struggle a political character.[9]

As the political struggle of the oppressed classes in Syria grew and spread throughout the country, the conservative forces allied with the United States and rightist elements within the military pressed forward to consolidate their hold through another camp led by Col. Shisakli in 1951, who tightened his reign through a right-wing military dictatorship. As part of his strategy to halt peasant unrest, "Shisakli directed a pitiless repression against the peasants. The gendarmerie and army forces evicted peasants from their villages and expelled them from their home districts. Thousands of peasants were imprisoned and many were tortured."[10]

The continued unrest and political upheaval in Syria during this period, however, kept up the momentum against the regime and forced it to come to terms with the impending crisis. As a result, in 1954 the military high command was forced to resign and the Shishakli military dictatorship was toppled.

The transition to electoral politics and the role of political parties in national political activity during the late 1950s—especially the Ba'th Party and parties affiliated with trade unions and other labor organizations, such as the Communist Party—set the stage for the transformation of the Syrian political economy, pressing the state to play an active progressive role in the national economy. With the resurgence of nationalism in the Arab world in the aftermath of the Suez crisis, the petty-bourgeois nationalist forces in control of the Syrian state launched in the late 1950s a national, state-capitalist policy that came to define the course of economic development in subsequent years. This process opened the way to the union with Egypt (another nationalist, state-capitalist regime) through the formation of the United Arab Republic (UAR) in 1958.[11]

> On 1 February 1958 Presidents Nasser and Quwatli proclaimed the formation of the United Arab Republic. It was a move into the unknown made in the heat of enthusiasm. The joint communiqué declared: "In proclaiming these decisions, the participants feel great pride and overwhelming joy in having assisted in taking this positive step on the road to Arab unity and solidarity."[12]

The union of Egypt and Syria promised to bring together two strong Arab states and thereby cement the bonds of Arab nationalism. The union agreement was approved by a referendum in both countries, and Nasser was elected president of the new UAR. Soon after, "Nasser visited Damascus and was given an overwhelming welcome. Thousands came into the streets to greet him, the most popular Arab leader ever, and Arabism was at its zenith."[13]

Underneath all this euphoria, however, all was not well with the union as originally conceived: "The UAR was to consist of two regions—the northern and the southern—with Cairo as capital. And here was the root of future problems—the unequal relationship and Egyptian insensitivity."[14] In demanding a total union under Egyptian dictates, Nasser was able to impose his own terms on a fragile alliance that was uneven from the very start:

> He demanded total union, the abolition of all political parties except his own National Union and the Syrian army's abstention from politics. . . . In addition to the dissolution of Syrian political parties, army officers were dismissed and Egyptian security officials sent to Syria.

> . . . [I]n October 1958 in a new cabinet 14 out of 21 minis-
> ters (including the most important) were allotted to Egyptians.
> Nasser's other moves alienated a considerable section of the
> population—landowners who disliked the plans for agrar-
> ian reform, politicians who lost power, businessmen and the
> army.[15]

Over the next three years, there was discontent in the Syrian
army, despair among members of the Ba'th, and general dis-
illusionment among the Syrian people toward this lopsided
merger. Clearly, the imposition of centralized rule from Cairo
to cope with the problems of the union was no solution at all.
The stage was thus set for the Syrian army to move in: "On 28
September 1961 army units stationed outside Damascus
marched on the capital where they were joined by others and a
national uprising was proclaimed."[16] Thus, the union came to
an end. The merger of the two countries had lasted only three
years.

Within one and a half years of the end of the UAR episode,
the Ba'thist forces in Syria reorganized. They succeeded in
retaking power through the military coup of 8 March 1963.
Although the Ba'th's role in the coup was minimal or nonexist-
ent at the beginning, the rightist separatist elements within Ba'th
came to play an important role within the state structure soon
after the military established its hold on state power. Efforts to
reexert Nasserist control over the state through two attempted
coups (one in April and another in July) failed. The results of
the second were disastrous, as at least seventy people were killed
and many more wounded, while several of the ring-leaders were
executed.[17]

Increasing conflict between the radical nationalist and conservative reactionary factions of the Ba'th regime led to open
confrontation between the supporters of each side in a number
of major cities across the country. This prompted the radical
nationalist wing of Ba'th to stage a coup in February 1966 to
neutralize the reactionary forces among its ranks and to move
Syria more firmly along the state-capitalist path. The coup, which
was Syria's thirteenth and bloodiest army coup in seventeen
years, was led by officers loyal to Generals Jadid and al-Asad.

This "neo-Ba'thist" coup, which overthrew the rightist government headed by President al-Hafiz, shifted state policy in a nationalist direction.

With the radical wing of Ba'th in power, the nationalist forces once again pressed for the implementation of new economic policies to deepen the state-capitalist project. The government began to limit the role of private capital within the Syrian economy and initiated a series of laws to carry out the nationalization of local firms and to assure greater state control of the national economy. This was accompanied by a new land-reform law that promised the redistribution of land to landless peasants to increase production in the agrarian sector. While these measures were a reflection of the policies of the radical wing of the Ba'th government in power, other conservative elements within Ba'th fought to preserve private property rights and attempted to strengthen the private sector by limiting the role of the state in the economy.[18]

The conflict within Ba'th's radical and moderate factions on the question of how far to move on the state-capitalist road led to rivalry between them and to the coup of 1970, when the moderate wing of the Ba'th led by General Hafez al-Asad overthrew the regime.[19] Soon after taking power, General al-Asad had the whole of the old Ba'thist left wing arrested, including President Atassi, and consolidated his power as head of state.

Following its accession to power in 1970, the al-Asad regime began to ease restrictions toward private capital in an effort to enlist the private sector to take an active role in the Syrian economy. The state's liberalization policies beginning in the 1970s created great incentives for private capital in various branches of the local economy. With the relaxation of state control and regulation over production, commerce, and finance, private capital began to expand in all directions.

> Restrictions on foreign trade were relaxed. Syrian importers were given the right to import foreign products on their own account and directly from exporters. . . . Free trade zones were set up in different parts of Syria to enhance private-sector trade.
> In the hope of replenishing diminishing foreign exchange

reserves, Assad offered inducements for emigrants to repatri-
ate their capital. He appealed to exiled businessmen to come
home, promising them immunity from punishment for
smuggling out their capital, special facilities, and attractive
investment opportunities.[20]

Such policies provided the material basis for the expansion of
commercial capital and the development of a local comprador
bourgeoisie during the 1970s.

Although Syria has been developing in a private-capitalist
direction over the past several decades, the state's role in overseeing the economy has not totally disappeared. Some state-
capitalist practices continue to function within the broader
framework of a national economy that is part of the world capitalist system dominated by the imperialist states.[21]

Despite the internal power struggles between rival radical
and moderate factions within the Ba'th, and the signs of a
reversal of the state-directed economic policies of the past four
decades, Syria has managed to maintain a facade of an independent nationalist state. Nevertheless, developments of the past
decade point to a process of transformation similar to that in
Turkey and Egypt, where evolution along the state-capitalist
path in an earlier period resulted in the transformation of these
regimes into neocolonial satellites of imperialism.

Imperialism and the Nationalist Response
in Iraq

Prior to World War I, Basra, Baghdad, and Mosul were provinces
of the Ottoman Empire. With the collapse of the Ottoman
Empire at the end of the War, Britain took control of this territory to gain access to oil and other raw materials in the Persian
Gulf. Through its possession of this oil-rich region, Britain was
able to consolidate its hold on the Middle East.[22]

The collapse of the Ottoman Empire and the victory of the
British forces from Palestine to Iraq allowed Britain to remain
in the region and turn the Middle East into a vast British colony.
To assure its control over this territory, Britain, under a League

of Nations mandate, installed a monarchical government in Iraq that included pro-British local officers from the Ottoman army, leading merchants, and local bureaucrats with ties to the shaikhs and the landlords in the rural areas. The British-installed monarchy thus came to carry out the political and economic objectives of the British Mandate in Iraq and to safeguard British interests in the region well into the twentieth century.[23]

Imperialist domination of Iraq and its incorporation into the British-controlled world economy brought about a major transformation of the economy and society:

> Modern Iraq—its state apparatus, its social and economic character—had its beginnings in the early phase of European penetration . . . and its fitful but persistent integration into the world economy. This provoked a distinct shift from prevailing pastoral and subsistence agriculture to production for the external markets of British India and Europe, and transformed, over many decades, the relationship of shaikh and tribesperson into one of landlord and peasant/serf as communally farmed lands became the private estates of large shaikhs, urban merchants, and state officials.[24]

In line with this transformation, the colonial regime in Iraq turned the state into an instrument of imperial rule to fulfill the dictates of the British-controlled world economy. In this sense, the formation of the modern Iraqi state "was dictated by European convenience and the imperative of foreign [British] capital in consolidating its rule. Oil—the reserves of Mosul and proximity to the Persian fields—was the incentive for British control."[25]

The onset of the Great Depression and the sharp fall in world prices for Iraq's chief exports brought about an economic and political crisis that led to formal independence in 1932. The expansion of industrial and commercial activity during the 1930s and 1940s brought into being newer social forces, including a small working class and a more numerous middle class.

> The local bourgeoisie was overwhelmingly mercantile, closely tied to foreign capital and the landowners. The construction

of railways and ports, the growth of trading activity and work-
shops, and the expansion of the state apparatus brought into
being newer, urban-based social forces; a small proletariat,
and somewhat more numerous petty bourgeois and intermediate strata.[26]

Excluded from centers of political and economic power, and
subordinated to the dictates of the monarchy propped up by
British imperialism, these sectors came to articulate widespread
resentment of foreign control and local ruling-class collaboration with the imperialists. This led to numerous clashes between
the state and various segments of Iraqi society, including a
series of tribal rebellions in the 1936–41 period.[27]

The outbreak of World War II gave Britain the opportunity
to intervene in Iraqi politics, but this made matters worse, as
intensifying anti-British sentiment sparked a series of strikes,
demonstrations, and clashes between the workers and the
authorities.

> In July 1946, a strike took place in the Iraq Petroleum Com-
> pany, where permission to form a union had been refused; a
> strike meeting in Kirkuk was suddenly charged by armed
> police, and ten people were killed. . . . The killings at Kirkuk
> in July 1946 were a foretaste of the terrible violence of 1948,
> the year of the great national uprising known as *al-Wathba*,
> the leap.[28]

"The hatred revealed in the dreadful scenes in Baghdad on 26–27
January [1948]," write Marion Farouk-Sluglett and Peter Sluglett,
"was a portent of the wrath to come. . . . During the spring and
summer, violent opposition spread outwards from Baghdad."

> In what became the best-known uprising of that period, the
> IPC pumping station near Haditha was brought to a stand-
> still in April and May 1948 by a strike of the 3,000 workers
> and clerical staff, organized by the Communist Party. After
> two and a half weeks, the government and the IPC cut off
> supplies of food and water to the strikers, and after three
> weeks the latter decided to march to Baghdad, a distance of
> some 250 kilometers.[29]

"This act of defiance, known as *al-Masira al-Kubra*, the 'great march,'" note Sluglett and Sluglett, "was a major expression of popular determination to stand against the political order, even in the face of overwhelming odds."[30]

While mass repression against all antimonarchy and anti-British forces quelled efforts to overthrow the colonial puppet regime for the time being, the oil boom of the 1950s began to substantially transform the economic structure of the country in the direction of increased trade, construction, and manufacturing. Such expansion led to the emergence and growth of a national capitalist class whose interests were distinct from those of the old power block of comprador merchants and landlords that formed the power base of the monarchy.

The growth of industrial activity expanded the size of the working class and led to increased labor organizing by radical trade unions and political parties, such as the Iraqi Communist Party (ICP). The number of oil workers grew from 3,137 in 1941 to more than 15,000 by the mid-1950s, industrial workers numbered over 130,000 by 1954 (with more than 43 percent in establishments of over 100 workers), and the General Federation of Trade Unions claimed membership of some 275,000 workers.[31] With the growth of the working class in this period, the ICP became an influential political force among labor, organizing the largest and most strategic concentrations of industrial workers, especially in the oil fields.[32]

The growth of national capital and the aspirations of middle layers of society to nationhood and independence, the development of an increasingly organized and class-conscious working class, and the massive dislocation of peasants forced to migrate to the largest cities led to unrest in the army and resulted in the military coup of 1958 led by Colonel Abdul-Karim Qasim.[33]

In July 1958 the monarchy was overthrown. The ten years which followed can best be seen as a period in which those who had conspired to overthrow the monarchy vied for control of the republic. Significant social and economic reforms were undertaken; land reform was enacted, thereby striking at the power of the landowners who had kept the monarchy

alive, and the state took an increasingly active part in directing and controlling the industrial sector. The links which had
joined Iraq to the Western world were disrupted. . . .[34]

Representing the nationalist outlook of a rising national and
petty bourgeoisie, the Qasim regime set out to restructure the
economy on a state-capitalist basis that protected and advanced
the interests of the emerging national capitalist class.

The transformation of the class structure in Iraq following
the 1958 coup affected both the landowners and foreign capitalists, whose political power was broken. In line with the state's
nationalist economic policies, an agrarian reform program was
promulgated and the nationalization of oil was carried out during the 1960s. Soon, other sectors of the economy were affected
by the nationalization decree, when the largest manufacturing,
trading, and financial firms were transferred to the public
sector.[35] As Fran Hazelton points out:

> One of the main achievements of the Qasim period . . . was
> the agrarian law reform programme, largely a result of the
> ICP's efforts. This broke the political strength of the landlords.
> The power of the grande bourgeoisie was also broken at this
> time. Political and economic power were reconstructed in
> favour of the urban and petty bourgeoisie while maintaining
> the principle of private ownership. In addition to these inter-
> nal achievements Iraq's revolution cut the link with Britain
> and took Iraq out of the Baghdad Pact.[36]

While Qasim and the nationalist regime he headed helped
develop the basis of a national capitalist economy, the policies
enacted by the state during this period came into sharp conflict
with the interests of imperialism and local reactionary classes
that sought to oust him from power. The right-wing Ba'thists
proved to be instrumental in achieving their ends. On 8 February
1963 Qasim was overthrown by a violent, bloody coup led by
rightist Ba'thist forces—a coup that brought terror and death to
thousands of Iraqis.

"The Fascist coup of 8 February 1963, which brought the
Ba'th Party to power," writes U. Zaher, "was welcomed by all

reactionary forces and the enemies of the 14 July 1958 Revolution."

> The coup was marked by its extreme brutality towards the revolutionary forces which had played a principal role first in the struggle against colonialism and the monarchy and later for the defense and development of the July 1958 revolution.[37]

"The coup," Zaher goes on to point out, "was not merely reactionary. It was carried out to bring a fascist-style party, the Ba'th, to power."[38] He writes:

> The headquarters of the National Guard in all towns became torture centres. The National Guard and their Ba'thist masters viewed the Iraqi Communist Party as a special target for their countrywide barbarous crimes. . . .
> Armed with the names and whereabouts of individual Communists, the National Guards carried out summary executions. Communists held in detention . . . were dragged out of prison and shot without a hearing. . . . [B]y the end of the rule of the Ba'th, its terror campaign had claimed the lives of an estimated 3,000 to 5,000 Communists.[39]

The extremely anti-Communist nature of the ultrarightist Ba'thi regime during this period showed the class character of the Iraqi state as one violently opposed to the interests of workers and peasants, as well as all other progressive national forces, and supportive of a fascist bureaucratic-military elite.

The brutal rule of the Ba'th came to an end a mere nine months after they took power. On 18 November 1963, the military seized power in a coup that once again put the left-wing, petty-bourgeois nationalist forces back in control of the state apparatus. With the initiation of a nationalization policy similar to that of the Nasserist state in Egypt, the new military regime in Iraq played a central role in setting the stage for the development of a national state-capitalist economy during the course of its nearly five-year rule from 1963 to 1968.

The economic crisis of the mid-1960s, prompted by a drop in oil revenues, forced the regime to increase taxes while wages and salaries remained stagnant. Growing discontent with the policies of the military regime in power and its increasingly authoritarian rule gave the opportunity to right-wing military officers allied with the Ba'th to exploit the situation and to carry out a coup in July 1968 to restore Ba'thi rule—a coup that brought to power Ahmad al-Bakr and Saddam Hussein. Despite the change of regime, however, Iraq continued to develop along the state-capitalist path, which further strengthened the power of the bureaucratic elite under the watchful eye of the military.

In the period from 1968 on, further advances were made along the state-capitalist path when the number of agricultural cooperatives and collective farms grew, manufacturing industry expanded, and the share of the oil industry in the gross national product rose. Similar advances were made in construction, commerce, and services.

The industrial and commercial expansion of the 1960s and 1970s in Iraq led to the development of the local bourgeoisie tied to national industry. By the mid-1980s, the maturing national industrial bourgeoisie began to assert itself by demanding greater privatization of the economy and by opening up to ventures with foreign capital in both the Arab world and the West, thus integrating itself more and more into the world economy.

"The policy of promoting the private sector," notes Abbas Alnasrawi, "was further enforced with the introduction in February 1987 of an ambitious economic liberalization and privatization programme."[40] "The new measures," he adds, "represented a turnaround of the official ideology propounded since the Ba'th came to power in 1968."[41]

Among the changes effected by these new measures were the de-nationalization of key sectors of the economy, the reorganization of state-owned enterprises, and the encouragement of private capital:

> The main features of the new measures included selling state land, farms and factories to the private sector; encouraging private enterprise; and deregulation of the labour market by abolishing labour law. Other measures to benefit private enterprise included the reorganization of state enterprises and

restructuring of ministries and commissions, creation of companies to run state enterprises, enactment of laws to induce
the flow of Arab capital, introduction of limited competition
in banking, freedom to use foreign-held balances to finance
imports and the encouragement of private initiative in agriculture.[42]

The economic changes initiated by the state in Iraq over the
past decade or more have led to social and political unrest
among a growing segment of the population whose position
has not improved. This has led to political mobilization and
activity by various organized groups directed against the increasingly authoritarian state, which has become more and more
repressive.

The repression of the popular forces, the attack on the
Communists, and the exercise of dictatorial rule over the people
during the past two decades have coincided with the crisis of
the state-capitalist regime in Iraq in transition to a new stage of
capitalist development in the 1980s and 1990s. This development has further consolidated the state's firm grip over the
people and dragged the nation in an increasingly brutal, fascist
direction.

Conclusion

The experience of Syria and Iraq in national development in
the postindependence period was shaped by both internal and
external forces that played a decisive role in charting the destiny
of these two states in the postwar period. While the imperialist
control of Iraq and Syria during the British and French mandates
defined the parameters of national life under colonial conditions,
the internal class structure inherited from the earlier Ottoman
period, cultivated and reinforced by the Western imperialist
states to facilitate colonial rule, has become the determining
factor in postindependence political developments in these
countries right up to the present.

The rise of a nationalist movement based on the middle
layers of society, which came to power through an endless suc-

cession of coups and countercoups at various points in the evolution of the Syrian and Iraqi states over the past several decades, took place in the context of a postcolonial society with traditional (feudal and semifeudal) and modern (capitalist) class relations that the state in both countries came to confront. While a coalition of popular class forces have, at various points in the national struggle, fought against the dominant classes supported by imperialism, the petty-bourgeois-controlled state in both countries has not been able to (nor even wanted to) champion the national cause to benefit the laboring masses.

Whereas the right- and left-wing petty-bourgeois factions within the Ba'th leadership have failed in building a new egalitarian society in the postindependence period, they have likewise failed in fighting the forces of internal reaction, which have been propped up by imperialism to see the state-capitalist project succeed. The failure of state-capitalism in Syria and Iraq and the adoption by these states of an increasingly neocolonial position within the world economy is a logical outcome of the class project mapped out by the petty-bourgeois leadership that has chosen to remain within the confines of existing capitalist class relations.

5
The National Question in the Middle East

*The Palestinian and Kurdish Struggles
for National Self-Determination*

An enduring legacy of the Ottoman Empire since its disintegration and collapse at the beginning of the twentieth century has been the national question. The partition of the empire by the Western powers at the end of the First World War led to the fragmentation of the peoples of the Middle East, which created the Palestinian and Kurdish national questions.

The division of Ottoman territories on the southern flank of Asia Minor at the heart of the Fertile Crescent into a series of colonial outposts to advance Western geopolitical interests in the Middle East created an artificial interstate system that denied the Kurdish and Palestinian peoples their right to national self-determination. This historic denial of the right to a national homeland for the Palestinians and the Kurds prompted the emergence of the Palestinian and Kurdish national movements.

Palestine and the Palestinians

A prosperous, coastal province of the Ottoman Empire, Palestine came under British rule following the Ottoman collapse at the end of the First World War. The British Mandate, which controlled the territory stretching from Iraq to Jordan to Palestine, forced the native (Arab) population of Palestine to live under British dictates until the middle of the twentieth century.

With the arrival of a growing number of Jewish immigrants from Europe during the British Mandate, ethnic rivalry between Arabs and Jews reached new heights in Palestine. This rivalry was fueled by Zionist aims to secure a national homeland for the Jews in Palestine following the departure of the British from this territory. The British did leave, and the Zionists succeeded in establishing a Jewish state shortly after the end of the Second World War, but this also marked the beginning of the Arab-Israeli conflict centered on the Palestinian question—a conflict that stemmed from the dispossession of the native Arab peoples of Palestine.[1]

Under Ottoman rule, the Palestinians had largely been part of a rural, peasant population. "By far the majority of Palestinians in the nineteenth century, perhaps over 80 percent," writes Gordon Welty, "were peasants *(fellahin)*. Some cultivation was based on sharecropping, with a division of the agricultural product between peasant and the landlord of the state property *(miri)*. Much was based on peasant smallholding of *miri* land."[2] However, with the increasing commodification of agriculture, cash crops began to replace subsistence production. As a result, the rural social-economic structure began to undergo a process of transformation.

Not all Palestinians were tied to the agrarian sector, however; a small segment consisting of the privileged few lived in the cities: "[T]he cities were the home of the Palestinian elite (the *effendi)*—absentee landlords, religious officials, and various Ottoman state authorities—as well as, in the late nineteenth century, the intelligentsia."[3]

With the development of industry came a change in the structure of the labor force, as an increasing number of peasants sought wage-labor employment in the ever-expanding urban areas. Thus, by midcentury, the Palestinian population had become more diverse along occupational lines and increasingly urban.[4]

In the period following the establishment of the State of Israel, millions of Palestinians were driven into exile as refugees in neighboring Arab states. "Although some of the well-to-do Palestinians who enjoyed family or business connections in other parts of the Arab world had begun to leave Palestine shortly after the United Nations General Assembly called for the partition of the country in November 1947," writes Pamela Ann Smith, "the vast majority of the refugees left after fighting broke out between the Haganah—the underground Jewish army—and Palestinian irregulars, and later, after May 14, 1948, during battles between the Haganah, the Arab Legion (Transjordan), and the armies of Egypt, Syria, and Iraq."[5]

> Many initially sought safety in Lebanon, Syria, or other parts of Palestine, particularly during the heavy fighting in the Galilee in the Spring of 1948 and after the massacre of 254 villagers in Deir Yasin in April of that year. Others fled to the West Bank and Transjordan after the entry of the Arab Legion, seeking refuge in territories held by the Jordanian forces. Still others, including many from Jaffa and the southern coastal districts, sought the protection of the Egyptian army and fled to the Gaza Strip, or to Egypt itself.[6]

During this period, more than a million Palestinians took refuge in Jordan, while half a million were driven to Lebanon, over three hundred thousand to Kuwait, and nearly quarter of a million to Syria. Another half a million dispersed to the rest of the world, including several other Arab states, Europe, and the United States. Today, there are nearly 5 million Palestinians across the world, including over half a million in Gaza, over a million in the West Bank, and more than three quarters of a million within Israel itself.[7]

The overwhelming majority of the refugees from Palestine, notes Smith, "were either peasants who had owned their homes and land in Palestine, or tenant farmers and sharecroppers who had tilled plots in or near their native villages."

> Unlike those who had experienced urban life, received an education, or had business contacts abroad, the peasantry was uniquely deprived because its source of livelihood, the land, was lost. While a few were able to flee with livestock, household goods, and some agricultural tools, the lack of suitable agricultural land in the neighboring countries in which they

took refuge, combined with the relatively high rates of unemployment which already existed in the agricultural sector in the host countries, meant that most of the peasant refugees were unable to escape the poverty and loss of skills that confinement in the camps over the years, and even decades, entailed.[8]

"In contrast to the peasantry," Smith continues, "those Palestinians whose assets consisted of movable property or transferable skills were often able to make a new life in exile that, with time and effort, even surpassed the standard of living they had enjoyed in Palestine."

> As a result of the wartime prosperity which had resulted from the awarding of huge government contracts from the British, the beginning of oil exporting from Haifa, a significant rise in agricultural exports to Europe, and the development of corporate forms of business, many Palestinian merchants amassed considerable wealth in the form of stocks and shares, bank deposits, cash, and financial investments abroad.[9]

According to a survey conducted by the government of Palestine in 1946, the total amount of capital owned in Palestine in 1945 was about 281 million Palestinian pounds. Of this, £P 132.6 million was owned by the non-Jewish population—with £P 74.8 million invested in land, £P 13.1 million invested in agricultural buildings, tools, and livestock, and £P 44.7 million invested in industry, stocks, and commodities or invested abroad.[10] Thus, as Smith points out, "Some 44.7 million Palestinian pounds (U.S.$179 million at 1945 exchange rates) in capital, or about 16 percent of the total capital owned in the country, was held by the non-Jewish population in the form of assets that could be transferred abroad."[11]

> Balances held in sterling accounts in London were easily accessible to those forced into sudden exile, and the release of blocked accounts held in the Palestinian branches of Barclay's Bank and the Ottoman Bank following international negotiations in the early 1950s provided additional sums for

rebuilding lives in the diaspora. Some £10 million was estimated to have been transferred to Jordan in the form of bank
deposits and cash during the same period. (The magnitude
of such a sum can be gauged by the fact that this figure equaled
the total amount of money in circulation in the Hashemite
Kingdom at the time.)

These sums enabled many Palestinians to invest in new
businesses, or to re-establish their companies in neighboring
Arab countries.[12]

Thus, while exiled peasants and marginalized camp residents
provided the foot soldiers for the PLO in the liberation struggle,
the diasporan bourgeoisie played a key role in funding the PLO
to carry out its armed resistance. While the PLO's dispossessed
mass base maintained the organization's revolutionary posture,
the exiled prosperous sectors of the movement succeeded, through
their financial muscle, in exerting a conservative influence on
the PLO to keep it within the boundaries of established social-
economic relations. These contradictory tendencies within the
organization came to determine the class nature of the movement
as manifested at the highest levels of organizational leadership
and set the current context and future direction of the PLO as
an organization that is the expression of a national movement
struggling for liberation.

The Origins of the Palestinian National Movement

The Palestinian national movement emerged in the early twentieth century following the collapse of the Ottoman state during
the First World War. Although unrest in Palestine directed against
both the despotic Ottoman state and Zionist encroachments into
the region had begun earlier in the previous century, it became
further intensified during the British military occupation of
Palestine following the First World War. This was further fueled
by the creation of the State of Israel by the Western powers in
the aftermath of the victory over Nazi Germany at the conclusion of the Second World War.

The initial nationalist response to British occupation emerged from the discontent of the Palestinian masses against the structure of governance under colonial rule. This, coupled with the rise in Zionist armed provocations against the Palestinians during British rule, led to the strengthening of the Palestinian national movement.[13]

"As the Palestinian opposition became increasingly intense," writes Gordon Welty, "the British successfully pursued a policy of *divide et impera*."[14]

> British interests in Palestine were geopolitical—protecting the northeastern flank of the Suez Canal, which London viewed as the lifeline of the British Empire. The Ottoman general Jamal Pasha had shown the British in January 1915 that Palestine under hostile control could be the base of an attack on the canal. Those British interests were best served by a territory that was not ethnically so unified that the threat of self-determination was genuine.[15]

Thus, through the Belfour Declaration, Britain promoted the establishment of an independent Jewish state in Palestine, which would effectively divide the territory along ethnic lines, and in this way create competition and conflict between the Arab and Jewish communities for greater control over the region. British divide-and-rule policies, Welty points out, "were not limited to manipulating intercommunal tensions. They manipulated the competition among the Palestinian *effendi* as well."

> [I]t was Ottoman policy to balance the interests of the various Palestinian groups against one another. British policy intensified this competition by playing off one against the other. In particular, they pitted the Husseini family against the Nashashibi family, to the ultimate benefit of neither.[16]

The divisions promoted between Palestinian Arab elites, as well as between the elites and the masses, further intensified British control; but this also generated widespread resistance to colonial rule.

Palestinian resistance against the British Mandatory authority greatly increased in the early 1930s with the formation of the first exclusively Palestinian political party in 1932—the Istiqlal (Independence) Party. A general strike called in late 1933 led to direct confrontation and bloodshed. This was followed by the formation of a multitude of Palestinian political parties, including the Arab Party, the National Defense Party, and the National Reform Party. The unrest that ensued in the years following the political radicalization of the population led to the general strike of April 1936 and the Great Palestinian Revolt of 1936–39.[17] As Baruch Kimmerling and Joel S. Migdal point out:

> The Great Arab Revolt in Palestine, as Arabs have called it, was . . . the first sustained violent uprising of the Palestinian national movement, and the first major episode of this sort since 1834. . . . It mobilized thousands of Arabs from every stratum of society, all over the country, heralding the emergence of a national movement in ways that isolated incidents and formal delegations simply could not accomplish.[18]

However, Kimmerling and Migdal continue, "it also provoked unprecedented countermobilization."

> Astonished by its tenacity . . . the British poured tens of thousands of troops into Palestine on the eve of World War II. And the Zionists embarked upon a militarization of their own national movement—nearly 15,000 Jews were under arms by the Revolt's end. Inaugurating an increasingly militarist Jewish political culture, it contributed in the 1940s to a decision by Ben-Gurion and other Zionist leaders to prepare for military struggle against the Arabs rather than against the British.[19]

The British response to the rising tide of Palestinian nationalism included further arrests of Palestinian leaders and increased repression of the Palestinian Arab population. Meanwhile, Welty points out, Zionist terrorism mounted:

> Irgun (the self-styled National Military organization, which split from Haganah in 1935) began to bomb Palestinian civilian targets in 1938. As the Great Revolt wound down in late

1939, the Palestinians were carefully disarmed by the Mandatory authority—but the Zionists were not.[20]

This gave the impetus for the Zionists to further arm themselves and to prepare to seize state power. This effort resulted in the "mass expulsions of Palestinians from their homes and the destruction of their villages to clear the land for Zionist endeavors," says Welty, and violent acts of terror forced entire villages into submission. In April 1948, just prior to the end of the British Mandate,

> Irgun, under the leadership of Menachem Begin, massacred 254 Palestinian men, women, and children at the "pacified" village of Deir Yassin near Jerusalem, and then stuffed the mutilated bodies down the village wells in an exercise in ritual pollution. Subsequently, the Zionists publicized the atrocity and promised more; the Palestinians began to flee their homes en masse.[21]

Soon after this atrocity, war broke out between the Zionist and Arab forces, which further led to the displacement of more than seven hundred thousand Palestinians. The total number of displaced Palestinians, who dispersed to the neighboring Arab states, constituted 60 percent of the 1.3 million Muslims and Christians who had resided in Palestine before 1948.[22]

> The 1948 War is called al-Nakbah (the Catastrophe) by the Palestinians, an apt characterization. Their community was shattered, the people who fled the Zionist terror were consigned to refugee camps in Lebanon, Jordan, and Gaza, hundreds of Palestinian villages were obliterated—razed to the ground—and those Palestinians who were permitted to remain within Israel after 1948 were subjected to military occupation.[23]

Thus, through this process of displacement and rule by a colonial-settler state, the Palestinians were forced to surrender their national identity and were turned into a minority in their own native homeland.[24]

Palestinian Nationalism and the Struggle for National Liberation

During the 1950s and 1960s, Palestinian nationalism took expression through the actions of several liberation organizations that operated in the diaspora. These included the Arab Nationalist Movement (ANM), founded by George Habash in the early 1950s, and El Fatah, founded by Yasser Arafat in the late 1950s. Later, in the mid-1960s, the Palestinian Liberation Organization (PLO) emerged as an umbrella organization that brought together various political tendencies in the diaspora and defined the nature of the liberation struggle during the sixties.[25]

The emergence of the PLO and the continued presence of Fatah gave rise to the development of the National Front for the Liberation of Palestine, which engaged in military operations against Israel beginning in the mid-1960s. Armed actions by Palestinian commandos belonging to a number of other organizations were carried out against Israel throughout the 1960s.[26] Among these, the best known was El Fatah.

> El Fatah took the initiative in ignoring the clumsy machinery of the PLO and embarking on armed conflict as an avowedly national Palestinian movement independent of the Arab states. . . . The Arab states were opposed to such action to the extent that they did not feel ready for a military confrontation with Israel, or did not want such a confrontation.[27]

However, "as tensions between the Arab countries and Israel rose during the mid-sixties," writes Welty, "the liberation movement of the Palestinians in the diaspora reflected ambiguities that would only be resolved after the 1967 war."[28]

The defeat of the Arab states in the Six-Day War, which diminished the credibility of the Pan-Arabists within the Palestinian movement, and the purely nationalist and militarist nature of El Fatah, which lacked a mass base, led to the founding of the Popular Front for the Liberation of Palestine (PFLP) in late 1967.

The PFLP took a more sophisticated view of the liberation struggle: four forces opposed to Palestinian self-determination were now identified—the state of Israel, the world Zionist movement, world imperialism led by the United States, and Arab reaction.[29]

The PFLP, and later its breakaway group, the Popular Democratic Front for the Liberation of Palestine (PDFLP), became a direct rival of El Fatah, competing for support among the Palestinian masses. The sharp political focus of PFLP and PDFLP, with their Marxist-Leninist ideological orientation, served to differentiate them from other organizations within the Palestinian resistance. Within a short time, they came to play a prominent role within the mass movement.[30]

On a broader level, the PLO, by the early 1970s, had come to represent most of the Palestinian organizations active in the national movement. This was also a period of growth of the Palestinian movement and a period that witnessed increased discussion and debate among the various movement organizations on the future course of the resistance. While this strengthened the hand of the PLO and the Palestinian cause, it also posed a challenge to the Arab states, which wished to promote their own particular national interests—a development that led to open, brutal conflict between the PLO and some Arab states. It culminated in the 1970 Jordanian massacre that came to be known as Black September, when King Hussein's army unleashed a violent attack on the Palestinians to crush their growing power and influence in the country.[31]

The shifting of its base from Jordan to Lebanon following this massacre and expulsions from Jordan did not end PLO's misfortunes, however, as it became embroiled in the Lebanese Civil War in the mid-1970s. While the left wing of the movement supported the progressive forces led by Kamal Jumblatt and the Lebanese National Front, others chose to remain outside the conflict to avoid another Jordan. Nonetheless, the PLO could not divorce itself from the ongoing war in Lebanon, which for nearly a decade consumed its efforts and set back the movement by many years.

The entanglement of the PLO in the Lebanese Civil War, and its strategic position in Lebanon as a base for its political-military actions against Israel, cost the PLO another defeat when Israel invaded Lebanon in 1982.[32] The expulsion of the PLO leadership from Lebanon that followed intensified the repression of Palestinians in the Occupied Territories and resulted in the massacre of thousands of Palestinians in the Sabra and Shatila refugee camps in Lebanon, a massacre designed to wipe out the last vestiges of PLO influence in the country.

Despite all the setbacks and defeats suffered by the PLO during the 1970s and early 1980s, the nationalist movement maintained its momentum in continuing its struggle for national self-determination. The repression of the Palestinian people and their leadership in both Lebanon and the Occupied Territories in the aftermath of the invasion of Lebanon did not deter them from fighting for their legitimate rights.[33] In fact, such repression increased their resolve to rise up against the forces of oppression in mass protest. In the great Palestinian uprising of 1987 (the Intifada), tens of thousands of Palestinians rose up in Gaza and the West Bank against Israel's repressive rule in the Occupied Territories.[34] This popular, mass uprising within the boundaries of post-1967 Israel strengthened the case of the Palestinian movement in demanding a permanent solution to the occupation through local self-rule.

Such an agreement was in fact reached by the mid-1990s, when the governance of the Occupied Territories was transferred to the Palestinian authority. But the limited nature of Israeli concessions in recognizing local autonomy in Gaza and the West Bank, as well as the continued buildup of new Israeli settlements there, have complicated the prospects for a long-term peaceful solution to the Palestinian question.

Palestinian nationalism and the Palestinian national movement have come a long way over the past few decades. Despite the deportations, massacres, and destruction they have suffered over the course of their struggle for a national homeland, the Palestinians have been determined to fight for their rights to achieve national self-determination for however long it takes to accomplish this goal.

Kurdistan and the Kurds

For centuries, prior to the onslaught of the Ottoman Empire, the Kurdish people had settled in what became a vital corner of the Middle East, stretching from the mountains and hills of eastern Anatolia to the northern edge of the Mesopotamian valley. The Ottoman invasion of this territory in the sixteenth century brought with it a social transformation over the course of the following four centuries that profoundly altered the structure of social relations in Kurdish society.[35]

> After the Ottomans conquered Kurdistan in the sixteenth century, they set up a vassal system throughout the Kurdish territories. This system remained in force later, albeit modified by changing historical circumstances. The tribal *aghas* (landlords) competed with each other for power and influence; a conflict by one with the central state was seen by his rivals as an opportunity for weakening him. These traditional rivalries determined later political alignments in both Iraqi and Turkish Kurdistan. . . .
>
> Thus, historical conditions favoring ethnic cohesion among the Kurdish people were present only in rudimentary form in Kurdistan before the creation of the modern Middle Eastern states.[36]

Following the collapse of the Ottoman Empire, the territory inhabited by the Kurds came under the jurisdiction of first the Western powers and later the states that were created following European occupation. Kurdistan in this way came under the eventual control of the newly emerging nation-states of Turkey, Iraq, and Syria, as well as Iran.

> The situation after the Ottoman capitulation was anything but favorable for the Kurds, as the main portion of Kurdistan remained under Turkish control. Kurdistan in Iran had already been under the rule of the Persians since 1639, and South Kurdistan, which was identical with the former Ottoman province of Mosul, came under British rule. Turkish Kurdistan and South Kurdistan became the scene of the failed attempts of the Kurds to achieve independence.[37]

Covering a land mass of some 410,000 square kilometers, the territory of Kurdistan is populated (as of the mid-1990s) by some 22 to 25 million Kurds who call it their homeland. With about half the total Kurdish population and nearly half the total territory of Kurdistan inside its boundaries (i.e., 194,000 square kilometers), Turkey has the largest concentration of Kurds in the Middle East, about 12 million, close to a quarter of the entire population of Turkey. The portion of Kurdistan in Iran accounts for some 125,000 square kilometers where between 6 and 7 million Kurds (or more than 16 percent of the total population of Iran) live. In Iraq, some 4 million Kurds (or 28 percent of the entire population of Iraq) live on 72,000 square kilometers of land. And in Syria, some 18,000 square kilometers are populated by about one million Kurds (i.e., 9 percent of the total population of Syria). In addition, a little over one million Kurds live in neighboring states, including the former Soviet Union and several Arab countries, while more than half a million Kurds live abroad (mainly in Europe, especially Germany), where they have settled as migrant laborers.[38]

Traditionally, the tribe has played a central role in Kurdish society and social structure:

> The Kurdish tribe is a socio-political and generally also territorial (and therefore economic) unit based on descent and kinship, real or putative, with a characteristic internal structure. It is naturally divided into a number of sub-tribes, each in turn again divided into smaller units: clans, lineages, etc.[39]

However, as Bruinessen points out, "Not all Kurds are tribal; in fact in some areas non-tribal Kurds form an overwhelming majority of the population."[40] Nevertheless, "tribal segmentation," notes Gerard Chaliand, "dominates the whole of [Kurdish] society, since even those who are not tribalized are subject to its rules."[41] In fact, "in nearly all cases," Bruinessen agrees, "they are (or were until quite recently) subjected politically and/or economically to tribally organized Kurds, so that tribal structure is, as it were, superimposed upon quasi-feudal dominance relations."[42]

"The picture of the wild, warlike, free Kurds promulgated

by European and American travellers, traders, and missionaries," writes Ferhad Ibrahim, "never corresponded with reality but rather was a part of the phenomenon of 'Orientalism'."[43] "Contrary to popular belief," Chaliand points out, "only a small fraction of the Kurdish population is nomadic."

> Most are farmers and, to a much lesser extent, stockbreeders. The mountains afford no more than a subsistence level economy, whereas the plains of Syria and Iraq provide good yields of grain. . . . As a general rule, in the mountain areas where traditional methods of farming are still used, the peasants own their land, whereas in the plains large landowners depend on tenant farmers and, increasingly, on agricultural workers.[44]

Kurdish society has undergone major social transformations during the past several decades. Its character has been changing from one tied to an isolated, semifeudal agricultural system to one tied to a capitalist, urban-industrial structure based on wage labor:

> During the last twenty years, Kurdish society has undergone profound changes which have considerably altered its traditional structures. Feudalism has broken down, nomadism has disappeared and even semi-nomadism is now practiced by only a few thousand people. As agriculture is gradually mechanized the countryside is becoming depopulated; hundreds of thousands of peasants have poured into the Kurdish towns and the big Turkish industrial cities. . . . Contact with the world of the proletarians and with progressive intellectuals is politicizing them very rapidly.[45]

The great majority of Kurds are Sunni Muslims who follow the Shafi'i school, as opposed to the Hanafite school followed by the Turks and the Arabs. However, there are Kurds who follow the teachings of the Shiite sect (especially those who live in Iran, and some in Iraq), while others are followers of the Alevi and Yezidi religions.

The Kurds have a distinct language of their own, in both

spoken and written form, but its use has been banned in many of the countries populated by the Kurds. The most notorious among these has been Turkey, where the use of Kurdish to communicate in any form has been illegal and severely punished until recently. The ban on the use of the Kurdish language had stemmed from the policy to limit or block communication among the Kurds, as well as to erode their cultural identity to better assimilate them into the dominant culture and society.[46]

Variations in dialect and in written language practiced by the Kurds in Iran, Turkey, and the Arab states has been an obstacle to communication across national boundaries:

> There is a large number of different dialects which may be classified into a number of more or less distinct groups that are not, or only very partially, mutually understandable.
>
> 1. The northern and northwestern dialects, usually called Kurmanji (a potential source of confusion is the fact that some southern tribes also call themselves Kurmanj and consequently their language, Kurmanji, although it belongs to the southern group).
>
> 2. The southern dialects, often called Sorani, although Sorani properly speaking is only one of the dialects belonging to this group, which also includes Mukri, Sulaymani, and many other dialects.
>
> 3. The southeastern dialects, such as Sine'i (Sanandaji), Kermanshahi and Leki. These dialects are closer to modern Persian than those of the other two groups.
>
> These dialect groups show not only considerable lexical and phonological differences but also differ significantly in certain grammatical features. . . . Besides these three groups of proper Kurdish dialects, we find two other groups of dialects spoken in Kurdistan that belong to another branch of the Iranian family . . . Zaza and Gurani. . . . It should be noted, however, that no strict boundaries exist. Dialects merge gradually; groups speaking one dialect may live among a majority of speakers of another.[47]

In addition to variations in dialect by region, there are differences in written language, as exemplified in the use of a variety of alphabets:

The Persian-Arabic alphabet was used by all literate Kurds until the end of the First World War. Then, in the 1920s, the Bedirkhan brothers introduced the Latin alphabet, which became standard in Turkish and Syrian Kurdistan. In Iranian and Iraqi Kurdistan the Arabic alphabet was adapted to the peculiarities of the Kurdish language. In the former Soviet Union the Kurdish language was written in Cyrillic letters. The variety of alphabets and the lack of uniform Kurdish language has made intellectual communication among Kurds difficult.[48]

Despite these differences and the various cultural restrictions imposed upon them, the Kurds have resisted the oppression they have suffered at the hands of repressive authoritarian regimes that rule over the Kurdish territory, and have found ways in which a common bond can be developed among all Kurds in their struggle for national autonomy.

The Origins of the Kurdish National Movement

The Kurdish national question, and the origins of the Kurdish national movement, goes back to the collapse of the Ottoman Empire at the conclusion of the First World War, which led to the partition of Kurdistan by the Western imperialist states. Subsequently, the territories inhabited by the Kurds were divided among several newly established nations that effectively dispersed the Kurdish population across parts of the Middle East.

Although the first step in the formation of the Kurdish national movement was the publication of the journal *Kurdistan* in 1898, the national liberation struggle waged by the Kurds did not fully materialize until after the partition of Kurdistan at the end of World War I.

In Iraq, the first Kurdish revolt against the British occupation of Kurdistan took place in 1919–20. The movement, led by Sheikh Mahmoud, aimed to create an autonomous Kurdish state, but failed to achieve it:

In 1918 in South Kurdistan, the head of the Order of Quadiriya Dynasty in Kurdistan, Sheikh Mahmud Barzanji, declared himself *hukmdar* (ruler) of Kurdistan. Initially the British administration in Mesopotamia tolerated the attempt of the Kurdish leaders to gain independence; it had not yet decided what was to become of Mesopotamia and South Kurdistan. But in 1919 the British deprived the *hukmdar* of his power, fearing that Sheikh Mahmud would present them with a fait accompli before they were able to decide the fate of the occupied region.[49]

Although the Treaty of Sevres provided a provision (Articles 62–64) for the creation of an independent Kurdish state on Kurdish territory, this never materialized.[50] The maneuverings of the Western powers, especially Britain and France, resulted in further transfers of Kurdish land to foreign hands and prepared the grounds for a second revolt led by Sheikh Mahmoud in 1923. This uprising, however, was crushed by the British Army, and the sheikh was exiled to India.

With the signing of the Treaty of Lausanne in June 1923, which superseded the Treaty of Sevres, a great portion of Kurdish territory was annexed by the new Turkish state and brought a considerable segment of the Kurdish population under its control. In early 1924, a Turkish decree banned all Kurdish schools, organizations, and publications, including religious fraternities and schools, greatly limiting the freedom of thought and association.[51] In response, "a broad-based resistance movement formed after it became apparent to the Kurds that the new Kemalist state was a Turkish state that would not permit ethnic pluralism."[52] This prompted another widespread uprising throughout Turkish Kurdistan beginning in early 1925. As in earlier cases, the uprising was brutally crushed.

In the latter half of the 1920s and throughout the 1930s, a series of new uprisings throughout Kurdistan laid the groundwork for the subsequent upsurge in nationalist activity and resistance:

From 1925 to 1939, the barbarities of the Turkish military forces in Kurdistan provoked constant revolts and peasant uprisings.

In 1925 there was the major revolt led by Sheikh Said, then the revolts in Raman and Reschkoltan, halfway between Diyarbekir and Siirt. From 1926 to 1927 it was the turn of the populations of Hinis, Vorto, Solhan, Bingöl, and Gendj to rise up against the Turks. 1928 saw uprisings in Sassoun, Kozlouk and Perwari. From 1928 to 1932 an organized insurrection broke out in the Ararat area. Finally, from 1936 to 1939 it was the inhabitants of the mountains of Dersim who were battling against the Turkish troops. Apart from the Ararat revolt and the one led by Sheikh Said, these were all local and spontaneous rebellions.[53]

In the early 1930s, the uprisings in Turkey spread to the east across the border to Iran. In 1931, a new revolt broke out in Iranian Kurdistan under the leadership of Jafar Sultan, and a similar uprising in Iraq that year—first led by Sheikh Mahmoud (who had returned from exile in India) and later under the leadership of Sheikh Ahmed Barzani—set the stage for the mass confrontation with the British, who sent in the Royal Air Force to attack the Kurdish villages and put an end to the rebellion. Subsequent uprisings in Iraq in 1933 and in Turkey in 1936–38 were crushed, but increased nationalist activity in Iraq in the early 1940s led to further revolts in the period 1943–45.[54]

The defeat of these revolts and the retreat of the Kurdish leadership to Iranian Kurdistan led to the founding of the Kurdish Democratic Party (KDP) in Iran in 1945. A similar organization set up by the Kurds in Iraq (the Kurdish Democratic Party of Iraq) came to play a parallel role in coordinating efforts against the repressive state in Iraq.

Heightened nationalist activity and a series of uprisings in the region during this period opened the way to the proclamation of the first Kurdish Republic of Mahabad in Iran in early 1946. However, the new Republic, led by Qazi Mohammed, was destroyed merely one year after its inception.[55]

The defeat of the Mahabad Republic marked the beginning of the decline of the Kurdish national movement during the next two decades. It was not until the mid-1960s that the renewed struggle of the Kurdish national movement began to pose a serious challenge to the repressive regimes of the region ruling over Kurdish territories.

Kurdish Nationalism and the Struggle
for Self-Determination

Beginning in the mid-1960s and throughout the 1970s, the Kurdish movement experienced a resurgence. More and more various leftist political organizations came to embrace the Kurdish cause as part of their overall political strategy.

In Turkey, the organizations that incorporated the Kurdish question into their program included the Workers Party of Turkey and the Communist Party of Turkey.[56] Together with various Kurdish parties and groups active in Turkish Kurdistan, these and other leftist organizations played an important role in highlighting the Kurdish question during this period.

"In the 1970s," writes Martin van Bruinessen, "the Kurdish organizations competed in putting forward ever more radical demands. . . . Not only in the east, but all over Turkey, radical politics grew extremely violent."[57] Of all the active leftist political organizations in Turkish Kurdistan, the Workers Party of Kurdistan (Partiya Karkeren Kurdistan, PKK) was the most effective.

The PKK was founded by Abdullah Öcalan in 1978 and was active among workers and peasants throughout the Kurdish regions of eastern Turkey in the years leading to the military coup in 1980.

> The PKK's militant ideology and activities in the first two years after it was founded resulted in its rigorous persecution under the military regime. Most members of the PKK's Central Committee were not able to escape from Turkey after the coup in 1980. The arrest of part of the leadership was a heavy blow to the party. It was not until the mid-1980s that the PKK was again able to become active throughout Turkish Kurdistan.[58]

The military coup in 1980 was a great setback to the Kurdish struggle in Turkey, as the Turkish army launched a massive operation in the eastern provinces to break the back of the PKK and to neutralize the resistance movement across Turkish Kurdistan.[59] The military regime went all out to crush the

Kurdish movement in all major Kurdish towns and villages, imposing on them martial law and strict military/police control. As David McDowall points out:

> In order to contain this new serious challenge, the authorities resorted to a number of draconian measures to curb PKK insurgency. They embarked upon mass arrests following any guerrilla incident. The people of south-eastern Anatolia had been fearful of Turkey's armed forces ever since the establishment of the Republic, but a new phase of terror now began. Mass arrests took place, and beatings and torture became a commonplace experience among the Kurdish population.[60]

The situation created by this mass repression of the Kurdish population led to a paralysis of the Kurdish national movement in the early 1980s, but it did not last for long.

Countering the terror unleashed by the Turkish state, the PKK launched a guerrilla war to carry out a protracted armed struggle against the Turkish army. This action won the party the strong support of the Kurdish masses throughout Turkish Kurdistan.[61] By the mid-1980s, the PKK took center stage in the national struggle by founding the Armed Forces for the Liberation of Kurdistan and the National Liberation Front of Kurdistan, and called on all Kurdish organizations to join forces in support of the struggle for national liberation.[62]

In the late 1980s, there was a significant expansion of guerrilla operations across Turkish Kurdistan, which contributed to the growing sympathy and support for the PKK in Kurdish villages and towns. Mass demonstrations in support of the PKK took place in several towns—especially in the towns of Cizre and Nusaybin—in the Spring of 1990, and in towns across eastern Anatolia in March 1991. The demonstrations revealed the broad-based nature of PKK's political support.

> As in 1990 there were a number of clashes between civilian demonstrators and the security forces in Sirnak, Idil, Cizre, Midyat and elsewhere in early March 1991, and more demonstrations at *Now Ruz* (New Year) on 21 March, not only in Kurdistan but also in Adana, Izmir and Istanbul. In July 1991

... [there were] an estimated 20,000 protesters on the streets of Diyarbekir.[63]

PKK's role in these and other mass actions against the Turkish army's visible presence in the Kurdish towns has been central. Its mobilization of a large segment of the Kurdish population to fight state repression has gained the party recognition and respect throughout Turkish Kurdistan. In fact, as Martin von Bruinessen points out, "The PKK is the only Kurdish organization that has successfully challenged the Turkish army's domination of Kurdistan."[64]

"In the circumstances prevailing today," writes Ferhad Ibrahim, "the PKK considers violence to be the only form of resistance possible against the repressive actions of the Turkish state and the violence perpetrated by its local Kurdish agents, the aghas and the sheikhs."[65] PKK's armed actions against the Turkish state, which has used a large contingent of its army to put down the resistance in Kurdistan, have generated greater participation of Kurds in the PKK. But the capture by the Turkish authorities of PKK leader Abdullah Ocalan in 1999 has complicated the situation and thrown the PKK and the Kurdish movement in Turkey into great turmoil.

In Iraq, the Kurdish movement enjoyed a brief period of rejuvenation following the fall of the monarchy in 1958. This was largely due to the widespread backing and support the movement received from radical leftist parties, including the Iraqi Communist Party, as a way of forcing concessions from the new government. However, the Kurdish forces soon fell victim to the right-wing nationalist policies of the various Ba'th governments that came to power during the 1960s, especially after the fascist coup in 1963. The situation did not get any better after Saddam Hussein's accession to power in 1968, and the movement experienced a steady decline during the 1970s and 1980s.

For a brief period in the mid-1970s, both the PUK and DPK conducted guerrilla operations against the Iraqi state, but by the late 1970s differences over ideology and strategic questions led to a major clash that brought the alliance to an end. It opened the way to all-out government retaliation in which Kurdish villages were destroyed or depopulated in an attempt to isolate the guerrillas from their mass base in the rural areas.

"Beginning in the late 1970s," writes Ibrahim, "four events led to fundamental changes in the Kurdish national movement across Kurdistan: the collapse of the movement in Iraq; the Iranian Revolution of 1979; the military coup in Turkey in 1980; and the Iran-Iraq war, which raged on for nearly a decade."[66]

During the 1980s, the Kurdish movement faced formidable central governments in Turkey, Iraq, and Iran. The September 1980 coup in Turkey placed Kurdish regions in eastern Anatolia under martial law, and the Islamic Revolution in Iran in 1979 and the Iran-Iraq War that started in 1980 forced the movement into retreat during the 1980s.

In the months following the Islamic Revolution, "there were violent clashes between Kurdish nationalists and supporters of the Islamic regime."

> The army and Revolutionary Guards occupied the cities and towns, killing hundreds in the first battles, while many others were executed after summary revolutionary "justice." Thousands of armed Kurds took to the mountains and successfully engaged the army and Guards in guerrilla warfare.[67]

The predicament of the Kurdish people in Iran was thus no better than what their counterparts had experienced in Turkey and Iraq. And the ensuing Iran-Iraq War pitted the Kurds of one country against those of another. Thus, when Iran unleashed its violent attacks on its Kurdish minority in Iranian Kurdistan, the KDP-Iran sided with Iraq for financial and logistical support; conversely, when the Iraqi Kurds were being oppressed by the regime of Saddam Hussein, Iran gave increasing support to the DPK-Iraq in its effort to topple the Iraqi regime.[68]

As the Iran-Iraq War was winding down, the event that drew international attention to the oppression of the Iraqi Kurds was the Halabja massacre. The Iraqi government's chemical bombardment of the town of Halabja resulted in the deaths of thousands of Kurdish civilians. "Less than half a year later," writes Bruinessen,

Iraq once again used chemical arms against its Kurdish citizens, and it has effectively used the threat of such weapons of terror ever since. Not long after a ceasefire with Iran was signed, the third and most brutal *al-Anfal* offensive took place (in August 1988). It was directed against the districts controlled by the Kurdish Democratic Party, in the northernmost part of Iraq. Poison gas was used in the attack, killing thousands and causing the survivors to flee in panic.[69]

By the war's end, the Kurdish movement was in disarray in all three countries. Paralyzed and in the worst shape ever in its decades-long struggle for independence, the movement was to face yet another setback with the onset of the Gulf War of 1991. Following Iraq's invasion of Kuwait and its subsequent defeat after massive U.S. intervention, the Iraqi Kurds were encouraged to rise up against the regime of Saddam Hussein. The opposition forces that rose up ranged from Kurdish nationalists to Shiite fundamentalists to bourgeois liberals. However, as Bruinessen points out, the planned uprising completely backfired and led to the biggest disaster yet in Kurdish history:

> [I]n March 1991, the Iraqi Kurds rose up in the most massive rebellion ever. . . . For a few weeks, a feeling of freedom prevailed; the Kurds dismantled the existing government apparatus in the north, Iraqi soldiers surrendered to the Kurds or simply went home. But then it suddenly became painfully clear that Saddam's military power had not been destroyed in the war, as had been hoped. Iraqi tanks and helicopter gunships attacked the rebellious towns. Bombardments with phosphorous and sulphuric acid, and the fear of Iraq's formidable chemical arsenal, quickly demoralized many of the Kurds, sending hundreds of thousands in panic into the mountains and towards the Turkish or Iranian borders. More than two million people—half or more of the Iraqi Kurds— fled from their homes.[70]

The cross-border mass exodus of Kurdish refugees from Iraq to Turkey and Iran effectively internationalized the Kurdish question once again, forcing the three governments to address the impact of this crisis on their internal policies regarding their Kurdish minorities.

In the years following the Gulf War through the late 1990s, the Kurdish parties and mass organizations have regrouped and reevaluated their role in the national struggle. While variations in ideological positions continue to set apart the numerous Kurdish groups across Kurdistan, one common goal has always emerged as the binding principle that defines Kurdish identity: the collective struggle for national liberation, for a free and independent Kurdistan.

Conclusion

The displacement of the Palestinian and Kurdish peoples by the Western imperialist powers through the partition of the territories in which they lived in the aftermath of the collapse of the Ottoman Empire has been at the root of the Palestinian and Kurdish national questions. The oppression of Palestinians and Kurds in the occupied territories, where they have been reduced to an ethnic minority, is a direct outcome of an imperial policy that resulted in war, rebellion, and political turmoil throughout the Middle East during much of the twentieth century.

The partition of Palestine and Kurdistan, as well as the rest of the Middle East that fell under British and French rule, effectively dispersed or divided these two peoples from their historic homelands, subjecting them to the whims of newly emergent postcolonial states that came to power in the aftermath of the First World War or following the British and French Mandates: Turkey, Iraq, Syria, Lebanon, Jordan, and Israel. All were created under imperialist treaties that parceled out occupied Ottoman lands among the Western powers that came to rule over the peoples of the Middle East, including the Palestinians and the Kurds. And it is now in these independent Middle Eastern states that the Palestinians and the Kurds have been facing the most brutal oppression and are fighting for their national liberation.

The parallels between the Palestinian and Kurdish national struggles over the course of the twentieth century highlight the similarities in the experience of the two ethnic and national communities that have been victims of displacement and dispersion under the rule of dominant political forces for so long. These experiences led to the development of a national identity and national movement that became the expression of the communal will of the respective communities struggling to be free. The Palestinian and Kurdish national movements thus emerged in direct response to the forces that kept them down and relegated them to second-class citizenship in states hostile to their struggle for national autonomy and independence.

The national movements of both the Palestinian and the Kurdish peoples thus came to represent their aspirations for nationhood and free development of their language, culture, and very being in a setting that promoted all that they stood for as a people. But the internal divisions along class and ideological lines were at once a divisive *and* a unifying expression of a maturing movement that focused on the social and political forces that would lead their people to victory in the next phase of the national struggle.

The continuing struggles of the Palestinian and Kurdish peoples in the face of much adversity is a testimony to the national aspirations of these and other oppressed peoples throughout the Middle East who are determined to fight for their right to nationhood and national self-determination until their final victory.

6
The Arab-Israeli Conflict

*War and Political Turmoil in
the Middle East*

The hotbed of imperialist rivalries, war, occupation, and political turmoil in the twentieth century, the territory stretching from Asia Minor to the Nile Delta and from the Fertile Crescent to the shores of the Eastern Mediterranean became the predatory playground of the Western imperialist states. Their legacy in the aftermath of the Second World War has been the postwar Arab-Israeli conflict, which has afflicted the region with crisis and turmoil for more than half a century.

The Origins of the Arab-Israeli Conflict

The imperialist states needed to establish an imperial outpost capable of responding to the changing needs of a global capitalist empire dependent on oil to fuel its industrial might in the advanced capitalist centers of Europe and the United States. The creation of the State of Israel became a convenient geopolitical strategy for the imperialist states to dominate the entire Middle East region in the postcolonial period following the Second World War.[1] The coincidence of the Nazi persecution of European Jews and the creation of the State of Israel in 1948 served well the needs of the imperialist states to maintain their foothold in this part of the world in close proximity to sources of oil in the Middle East.[2]

The imperialist scheme to establish this European outpost in the heartland of Arab culture and society, however, led to the displacement of the native population of Palestine, which came in the wake of the establishment of the State of Israel and the first Arab-Israeli War that resulted from it. The wholesale transfer of Palestinian land into the hands of Jewish settlers created a massive dislocation and raised social tensions between the Palestinians and Jews, who found themselves in rivalry for land, resources, and control over these territories.[3] Deprived of their political power and social rights, and finding themselves in the midst of a global chess game used to protect and advance the economic and geopolitical interests of the imperialist states through their surrogate, Israel, the Palestinian Arabs became minorities in their own land and were forced into exile as refugees in neighboring Arab states.[4]

> The Zionist dream of de-Arabizing the country and realizing a clear Jewish majority finally came about during the 1948 war, when 750,000 Palestinians, or more than 80 percent of the Arab inhabitants of what became Israel, took up the road of exile. Commenting on the exodus, Chaim Weizmann, by that time the first president of the State of Israel, proclaimed the Arab evacuation to have been "a miraculous clearing of the land: the miraculous simplification of Israel's task." It was, in fact, less of a miracle than it was the culmination of over a half century of effort, plans, and (in the end) brute force.[5]

Referring to the works of two Israeli historians—Meir Pa'il, historian of the Haganah and the 1948 war, and Benny Morris, who has written on the origins of the Palestinian refugee problem—as well as Ben-Gurion's multivolume *War Diary*, Masalha provides additional insight into Zionist plans to depopulate Palestine of its Arab inhabitants.

> Meir Pa'il . . . estimates that, of the total refugee exodus, "one third fled out of fear, one third were forcibly evacuated by the Israelis . . . [and] one third were encouraged by the Israelis to flee." . . . Benny Morris gives six major reasons for the abandonment of some 369 Arab villages: "expulsion by Jewish

forces," "abandonment on Arab orders," "fear of Jewish attack," "military assault on the settlement by Jewish troops," "whispering campaigns (i.e., psychological warfare)," and "influence of fall of, or exodus from, neighbouring town."[6]

"But what he [Morris] and Pa'il and other Israeli historians fail to acknowledge," Masalha adds, "is the pattern of these attacks and orders; they contend that the expulsion of the Arabs and the destruction of the villages were governed by strategic military considerations rather than any pre-meditated plan or design."[7] In fact, the expulsion of the Palestinian Arabs and the expansion of Jewish settlements into strategic points through-out Palestine was part and parcel of the plan (Plan Dalet) to expand the territory to be occupied by the new State of Israel once it was founded—a plan that was conceived several years prior to the 1948 war, and one that was part of the thinking of Ben-Gurion and other Israeli leaders, who saw the depopula-tion of Palestinian Arab villages and the acquisition of Arab lands as the only way to secure victory and assure the triumph of the Zionist state. Speaking to the Zionist Actions Committee on 6 April 1948, Ben Gurion declared:

> We will not be able to win the war if we do not, during the war, populate upper and lower, eastern and western Galilee, the Negev and Jerusalem area. . . . I believe that war will also bring in its wake a great change in the distribution of the Arab population.[8]

Yitzhak Rabin, former chief of staff and prime minister of Israel, summed up the matter directly when he said: "By razing villages to the ground and driving out the inhabitants we will ensure that there are no villages left for the Arabs to return to."[9] These views were put into practice by the new Israeli state in a very real way:

> After 15 May 1948, the Israeli army attacked countless defense-less Arab villages, blew up houses and entire villages and indiscriminately killed men, women and children. The survi-vors were driven out of the villages. News of these appalling

massacres spread like wildfire and those who did not believe
the reports were likely to become the next victims.
 The Israelis' psychological warfare was based on shock
tactics. Israeli radio was constantly calling on the Palestinians to flee "to avoid a bloodbath." Israeli army vehicles with
loudspeakers drove through the streets of towns and villages
pointing out escape routes.[10]

The displacement of the Palestinian population and its
dispersion to Jordan, Egypt, Syria, Lebanon, and other Arab
countries, and the denial to them of a national homeland and
self-determination to run their own affairs, led to the disintegration of Palestinian society, despite its nominal reintegration
into the social fabric of the states in which they built themselves
a new Palestinian identity.[11] The Palestinian diaspora became a
focal point of political resistance in those countries, as well as a
rallying point for the Palestinian resistance movement that
developed and spread to every corner of the Arab world.[12]

 The emergence of radical political organizations, such as
the PLO, during the ensuing period engulfed the Arab states in
Palestinian politics. All were forced to take an official stand
against Israel and its role as a surrogate of Western imperialism. Thus, the Palestinian question came to define the logic of
relations between Israel and the Arab states. As a result, the
Palestinian cause more and more became identified as the Arab
cause, and the liberation of Palestine became the single most
important rallying point of Arab nationalism.[13]

From the Six-Day War to the October War:
The Deepening Arab-Israeli Conflict

The Arab-Israeli conflict, which originated with the war of 1948
over the partition of Palestine and the establishment of the State
of Israel on Palestinian soil, was reinforced by subsequent
imperialist encroachments into the region (aided by Israel) that
led to the Suez War of 1956. The consolidation of Zionist power
in Israel during the 1950s and 1960s, and the expansionist nature

of the Zionist state in search of new land and resources for a greater Israel, led to the Six-Day War of June 1967—the third Arab-Israeli war in less than two decades.

The war, waged on several fronts—in the Sinai, the West Bank, and the Golan Heights—lasted no more than six days, and ended with the Israeli occupation of prime Arab lands. The speed with which Israel secured a ground and air victory over its more numerous Arab neighbors, with their much bigger armies, shocked the Arab world to its foundations.

The Israeli Defense Forces (IDF) annihilated the Arab air force within the first day of the outbreak of the war.

> On Monday morning, June 5, 1967, Moshe Dayan ordered the attack. Flying low to evade Egyptian radar, Israeli planes headed for Egypt's airfields. The Israelis destroyed the entire Egyptian air force while it was still on the ground. The planes, sitting wing to wing, had not even been camouflaged.[14]

Once this was accomplished, Israeli troops were able to capture the Egyptian Sinai, the Jordanian West Bank, and the Syrian Golan Heights a few days later.

> Without air cover Egyptian troops in the Sinai desert were vulnerable targets. Thousands of Egyptian soldiers were killed or wounded. Using the shield of Mirage jets, Israeli tank brigades pushed through the desert with lightning speed, despite some fierce fighting in the Gaza Strip by Palestinians attached to the Egyptian Army. . . .
>
> Even as the Egyptian Army was being defeated, tens of thousands of people throughout the Arab countries rallied to the fight against Israel. . . .
>
> Many people prepared for a long battle, confident of an Arab victory. They were stunned when, after only six days, the war ended in a humiliating defeat.[15]

By 10 June, the war was over. The Israeli victory brought with it the occupation of East Jerusalem, the West Bank, the Gaza Strip, the Golan Heights, and the Sinai. Thus, in a very short time, Israel had quadrupled the area of its territory.[16]

Humiliated in defeat, the Arab states searched for ways to explain their historic defeat and became more determined in linking their fortunes and national image to an official policy that identified Israel as the chief enemy of the Arab nation and the Palestinian cause, and Israel's Western allies—especially the United States—as the chief underwriters of Zionist aggression in the Middle East.

The defeat of the Arab states in the Six-Day War further contributed to the intensification of the Arab-Israeli conflict and prompted a militant anti-Israeli response by the Palestinian national resistance in the late 1960s and early 1970s.[17] Some militant factions within the PLO saw armed struggle as the only viable option to continue the resistance.[18] Clandestine guerrilla activity (including bombings, hijacking of planes, political kidnappings, and secret military operations) led by splinter groups of the PLO and other radical Palestinian organizations came to define the nature and scope of the Palestinian armed resistance in the period following the Six-Day War.

In the years immediately following the Arab defeat in 1967, the Arab states came to more readily embrace the Palestinian cause and allowed on their soil greater Palestinian militant activity directed against Israel—a move that led to an enormous growth in strength of the Palestinian national movement in many Arab states in the period following the Six-Day War. However, this newfound power of the Palestinian movement culminated in some countries in direct confrontation with the authorities, as in Jordan, where in September 1970 the Jordanian army was brought in to crush the PLO.[19]

While the state of war that existed between Israel and the Palestinian armed opposition characterized the late 1960s and the early 1970s as a period filled with tensions and crises, the next Arab-Israeli War of October 1973 and the subsequent Arab-led OPEC oil embargo against the West threw the entire region into a tailspin. The devastation caused by war and its political fallout set the tone for Arab-Israeli relations for much of the rest of the decade.

The October War was an outcome of the failure to resolve the Palestinian question and the fate of the Arab territories captured by Israel in the Six-Day War. The transformation of the Palestinian cause into an Arab cause, with Israel as an outcast that deprived the local inhabitants their rights to self-determination and nationhood, defined the new Arab will to champion a popular mission to unite the Arab world against a targeted enemy. Thus, the October War was to be an outlet for a larger political goal that, if successful, would have changed the dynamics of Arab politics throughout the region, and in this way restructure the terms of engagement between the opposing sides. But the outcome of the war was far short of what the Arab states hoped.

The October War began with the Egyptian tanks crossing the Suez Canal and plunging into the Sinai, while the Syrian army advanced into the Golan Heights. Following this, the Egyptian and Israeli defense forces came face to face in a major tank battle in the Sinai.

> On October 6, 1973, Egyptian troops launched a massive surprise assault across the Suez Canal, and Syrian tanks and soldiers stormed into the Golan Heights. Well-trained and well-equipped Arab soldiers drove back the Israeli occupiers in the initial fighting. Even the fiercest critics of Sadat in Egypt were caught up for a few days in the elation that swept the Arab capitals. Egypt and Syria were at last fighting for their land—and winning![20]

Well, not quite. The subsequent Israeli response to the Arab assault was prompt and began to turn things around in Israel's favor, but not before much blood was spilled:

> Israel mobilized rapidly for the counterattack, expecting a quick victory. Instead, the fighting was intense on both fronts. Israel suffered thousands of casualties and lost large numbers of planes and tanks. As the fighting continued, Israel attacked the Syrian capital of Damascus. To punish the Syrians, Zionist leaders decided to reduce much of the Syrian economy to rubble. The Israeli air force bombed ports, factories, power plants and oil refineries throughout the country and government buildings in the capital. These attacks killed many civilians.

As Israeli troops began to drive the Syrians back toward Damascus, the government formed popular militias to defend the city.[21]

In Egypt, the situation was quite different. Egypt's entry into the war through its direct action against Israel was more a political maneuver than a military one. The Egyptian decision to go to war to liberate the Sinai was a move calculated to put pressure on the major powers to force Israel to come to terms with the U.N. Resolution 242, which called for the return of all territories captured by Israel during the Six-Day War. Hostilities between the two countries did not end until well after the OPEC oil embargo against the West, and it took the two superpowers—the United States and the USSR—to draw up a ceasefire agreement, but the strategy succeeded in opening the door to bringing Israel to the negotiating table to settle the various central issues surrounding the Arab-Israeli conflict since the Six-Day War.

Ironically, the October War thus came to serve as a catalyst to bring the parties together for a peaceful resolution of the Middle East crisis. Nevertheless, it was not until the end of the 1970s that the warring parties seemed prepared to discuss the critical questions that separated them. These discussions ultimately culminated in the signing of a peace treaty between Egypt and Israel through the Camp David Accords in 1978–79 as the first step toward a comprehensive peace in the Middle East.[22]

While the return of the Sinai to Egypt some four years later, in 1982, reinforced the normalization of relations between Egypt and Israel and put an end to the state of war between them, the continuation of the Israeli occupation of the West Bank, Gaza, and East Jerusalem, and the repression of the Palestinian population in the Occupied Territories, failed to resolve the underlying contradictions that had given rise to the Arab-Israeli conflict.[23] The failure of the Camp David Accords to provide a viable solution to the Palestinian question, and the exclusion of Jordan and the PLO from the talks, thus effectively blocked the development of a comprehensive peace plan for the Middle East.

The Israeli Invasion of Lebanon and the
Disarming of the Palestinian Command

The failure to resolve the Palestinian question and to address the consequences of the Six-Day War—the return of the Occupied Territories captured by Israel during the war, which had not been settled by the October War of 1973—led to increased mobilization of the Palestinian forces in the late 1970s and early 1980s, especially in southern Lebanon.

By 1981, a series of crises had heightened tensions in the Arab world, especially in Syria, Iraq, and Lebanon: the missile crisis with Syria, the raid against the Iraqi nuclear center, the annexation of the Golan Heights, and the cross-border shelling between the PLO and the Israeli defense forces in southern Lebanon.[24] Although a cease-fire was negotiated later in the year, Israel moved its troops across the border into Lebanon to secure a forty-kilometer strip to prevent PLO shelling of Israeli villages. But the move into southern Lebanon did not stop at the security zone that Israel claimed to have established. The Israeli forces continued their advance into Lebanon and by late June 1982 were at the gates of Beirut.[25]

The siege of West Beirut was accompanied by a massive Israeli military assault that included widespread heavy bombing, including napalm and scatter bombs, that caused grave destruction and death throughout the Lebanese capital. As part of its "mopping up" operation to annihilate the PLO, Israel gave the green light to its Falangist allies to break the back of the Palestinian resistance.

On 16–17 September, the right-wing "Christian" Falangist militias, in collaboration with the Israeli army, carried out a bloody massacre of more than a thousand Palestinians in the Sabra and Shatila refugee camps in Beirut.[26]

> Early in the afternoon of 15 September 1982 the Israeli army used tanks and mortars to cordon off the Palestinian refugee camps of Sabra and Shatila in the south of Beirut. . . . *No one could get into or out of the camps without the permission of the Israelis.*

On the evening of 15 September, the Akka and Gaza hospitals were full of injured people. The Israeli army continued to fire sporadically on the surrounded camps. The following morning, local people were awoken by low-flying Israeli bombers screaming over the camps. It was 16 September. No one had any idea of the barbarity and cruelty that was to take place in the huts and ruins of this Beirut suburb in the next 48 hours.[27]

"According to the unanimous accounts of survivors," writes A. Frangi, "the militias, about 250 men at first, entered the camp from the south and south-west at around five o'clock on the afternoon of 16 September. The bloody massacre began in the Arsal district opposite Israeli headquarters."[28]

Descriptions of the cold-blooded murder of Palestinian residents in the two camps reveal the gruesome nature of the mass killing of innocent civilians over two long, horrifying days: "Friday was a day of unspeakable horror. The extent of the savagery and brutality cannot be described in words. This inferno stunned even the survivors into shocked silence. Yet the massacre continued with undiminished ferocity until late Saturday afternoon."[29]

The brutality with which the residents of the Sabra and Shatila camps were murdered during these two days sent shock waves throughout the world, and was reported in great detail in the press:

They shot anything that moved in the small streets. They smashed down doors and exterminated entire families who were eating their evening meal. People were killed in bed, in their pajamas or wrapped in blankets. Often the murderers were not satisfied with killing. In many cases, they cut off their victims' limbs before killing them. They smashed the heads of young children and babies against the walls. Women and even young girls were raped before being axed to death. Sometimes people were pulled out of the houses and summarily executed in groups on the street. With axes and knives the militias spread terror, indiscriminately slaughtering men, women, children and old people. . . .

In the Horch Tabet district of Shatila camp, the entire Mikdad family was murdered at the beginning of the massacre: 39 people, men, women and children, all massacred. This Lebanese family, originally from Kesseruane, had owned a garage in Shatila for over 30 years. Some had their throats cut, others had their bodies slit open, among them a 29-year-old woman called Zeinab. Her belly was cut open and the fetus put in the arms of the dead mother.[30]

Documenting the destruction and devastation suffered by the Palestinian residents in the two camps, Rosemary Sayigh writes: "From whichever route you chose into the Sabra/Shatila area following the massacre, you were immediately struck by the concentration of destruction. It was as if the place and its people had been the object of an attempt at total destruction."[31]

After the air, land and sea bombardments of the summer had come the Lebanese Special Units, programmed to slaughter and loot; and with them had come bulldozers which had cut broad swathes through housing, toppling breezeblock walls like cardboard. It was women who hunted through the ruins for bodies or scraps of possessions. . . . Most of the bodies had been taken away by 20 September, but the stench of death was still everywhere, and all the outsiders wore gauze masks.[32]

Once the massacre came to an end, one found nothing but mass destruction in the camps. The fascist Falangist militia and their Israeli allies had accomplished what they had set out to do. "It was not only the scale of the atrocity and destruction that made the scene so catastrophic," writes Sayigh, "but also its political message. Now the Resistance movement was gone: Palestinians in Lebanon and Lebanese who had supported them were at the mercy of the political forces whose character and intentions were signaled by the massacre itself."[33]

Despite the success of the Israeli defense forces in disarming and expelling the PLO from West Beirut and its military camps in southern Lebanon, the Israeli complicity in overseeing the massacre of Palestinian civilians—many of them women and children—in the Sabra and Shatila refugee camps created a new situation for the Palestinian resistance movement in Lebanon, a situation that facilitated Lebanon's Arab neighbor Syria's entry into the local scene.

The more direct intervention of Syria in Lebanese affairs in the period following the Israeli invasion resulted in the expansion of Syria's role in the country and led to the eventual end of the U.S. and Israeli presence in Lebanon in the 1980s. Despite continued incursions into Lebanese territory in the south, Israel could no longer see itself directly involved in the complex political and military mix of events in the turmoil that came to characterize daily life in Lebanon during and following the Israeli invasion.

The decade of the 1980s saw the development and spread of Islamic fundamentalism in Lebanon and elsewhere in the Middle East—a development that was an outcome of the Islamic Revolution in Iran in 1979.[34] Throughout the decade, militant Islamic groups, such as the Hizb'allah (the Party of God), spread in Lebanon and other Arab states, including the Occupied Territories of Gaza and the West Bank. While their increased presence in southern Lebanon helped facilitate the Palestinian resistance to Israeli incursions into Lebanese territory, right-wing fundamentalist organizations such as the Islamic Resistance Movement (Hammas) became instrumental in shifting the battle to Israeli soil.

Although their purpose was completely different than that of the United Patriotic Leadership under the PLO's command, the growing activities of Islamic fundamentalist groups in the Occupied Territories paralleled the renewed Palestinian struggle during this period and helped spread the anti-Israeli resistance that sparked the great Palestinian uprising (Intifada) in Gaza and the West Bank.

The Intifada and Renewed Conflict in the Occupied Territories

The Intifada, which took place on territories occupied by Israel since the Six-Day War, had a greater psychological impact on

Israeli society and on the future of the Palestinian question than any previous event; it profoundly altered the focus of the Arab-Israeli conflict and redefined the parameters of the peace process in the Middle East.

> In early December 1987 riots broke out in the Gaza Strip, accompanied by violent confrontations between Palestinians and the occupying forces of Israel. This was the start of what became known as the Palestinian Intifada or Uprising: a sustained attempt by the inhabitants of the occupied territories of the West Bank and Gaza Strip to throw off the yoke of Israeli occupation by means of mass protest and non-cooperation after more than 20 years of subjugation.[35]

"Palestinians by the thousands," writes F. Robert Hunter, "moved onto the streets of Gaza's teeming refugee camps to battle Israeli soldiers for control of their areas."[36]

> Surging crowds; PLO flags flying from rooftops and telephone lines; marches and demonstrations; hospitals filled to overflowing: these scenes were repeated in many places. . . .
> Commercial strikes also figured prominently in the first days and weeks of the revolt. These occurred not just in Gaza but all over the West Bank, in Jenin, Ramallah, al-Bireh, Nablus, Tulkarm, Bethlehem and East Jerusalem. All means were sought to keep the uprising going, to maintain its momentum.[37]

The Intifada was an expression of discontent among the Palestinian masses who would no longer bear the repression and humiliation suffered under the rule of an occupying army. "It was with a sense of nothing more to lose," write Ze'ev Schiff and Ehud Ya'ari, "that thousands of refugees grabbed at hoes, axes, sticks, stones, and whatever else came to hand to march out and proclaim that they would no longer stand for being treated like the dregs of humanity."[38] The Intifada was, therefore, a response of the Palestinian people who yearned to be free.

> [T]he Palestinian uprising against Israeli occupation . . . [occurred] nearly forty years after the partitioning of Palestine

and the creation of the Israeli state, and twenty years after the Six Day War and the Israeli occupation of the West Bank and Gaza. While during this time the Palestinians have always resisted Israeli rule, the *intifada* represents their first sustained, mass-based popular revolt. The duration, scope, innovative tactics, and accomplishments of the *intifada* make it a historic movement organizing Palestinian political unity around a clear and simple objective: ending the occupation and paving the way for self-determination.[39]

Thus, the process set into motion through mass, popular uprising showed that the only real solution to the Israeli occupation was the establishment of an independent Palestinian state in the Occupied Territories.

The uprising of 1987 in Gaza and the West Bank was the first step in recent years in the movement toward a Palestinian national homeland in the Occupied Territories, and the struggle surrounding this movement found in the Intifada a renewed determination to accelerate the momentum for a solution to the Palestinian national question.

[T]he Uprising, and the mass mobilization of the Palestinians which it had engendered, was more important than the rise of the PLO itself twenty years earlier and more important, too, than the rebellion of 1936–9 in the struggle of national independence. The Uprising had unified people to an unprecedented extent. Its direction, authority and impetus were rooted in the experience of the common people. This was a new sensation for Palestinian nationalism. The widespread civil disobedience was a people's war in a way the armed struggle had never been, and it commanded universal support in a way the Arab revolt of 1936 had failed to do.[40]

Thus, in this sense, write Samih Farsoun and Jean Landis, "The *intifada* is a historical product of all previous efforts to resist dispossession and suppression of Palestinian national identity. . . . The *intifada* represents the latest climactic expression of the collective Palestinian will, one asserting national consciousness, resisting dispossession, and reclaiming Palestinian political rights."[41]

The mass participation of the Palestinian population in the uprising showed the deep resentment that the people felt against the occupation and reinforced their will to fight back.[42] However, "Israel's decision to apply collective punishment techniques to the entire Palestinian population," writes Hunter, "arose from the failure of tough measures taken in late December, described at the time as the largest military sweeps since Israel took control of the occupied territories."[43]

> Mass arrests, curfews, house-to-house searches, road blocks, the blockading of entrances to refugee camps with barrels and barbed wire, a massive military presence (troop strength was tripled) and helicopters—as many as five over one area at a time—scattering tear gas canisters and smoke grenades over demonstrators had only led to greater outbursts.[44]

The determination of the demonstrators in putting up a heroic fight against the Israeli soldiers was a political act that was part of a broader strategy to achieve national self-determination.

> Facing the hot steel of M-16 bullets and choking under the stifling effects of tear gas dropped from helicopters or fired by soldiers, the demonstrators fought Israeli soldiers with brickbats, clubs, stones and petrol bombs. Youth with slingshots hurled marbles at low-flying helicopters. Protestors threw tear gas and smoke grenades back at the soldiers.[45]

Countering this mass struggle of the Palestinian people, Israel's response to the deteriorating political situation following the great Palestinian uprising was renewed expansion of the Israeli settlements in the West Bank. Coordinated to accommodate the large-scale migration of Russian Jews to Israel in the early 1990s, the new settlements became a permanent feature of Israel's expansionist policies in the post–Cold War era. While the building of settlements became a convenient way to solve Israel's housing-shortage problems, it also served to rationalize its colonial designs in securing ever-expanding borders. But such a "solution" did not go over well with the native inhabitants of these territories—the Palestinians—nor with some of the more radical Arab states. The tensions arising from such a situation have resulted in cycles of conflict and periodic eruptions that have heightened concern among progressive forces in Israel and in the neighboring Arab states over the past decade.

The fact that Israel has decided to proceed constructing new settlements in East Jerusalem throws a pall over the hope for a peaceful resolution of the national question. Indeed, if anything, such policy on the part of the Israeli government increases the likelihood of political crisis and runs the risk of prolonged military conflict.

7
The Gulf War

Interimperialist Rivalry for Control of Oil in the Middle East

Over the course of the past two decades the major imperialist powers of the late twentieth century (the United States, Germany, and Japan) have attempted to use as their surrogate one or the other of the chief regional powers in the Middle East (Iran and Iraq) to advance their political and economic interests in the region—above all, in securing access to sources of oil to fuel the industrial engines of their economies and thus maintaining global hegemony over their economic archrivals. In this inter-imperialist rivalry between the major capitalist powers of the world during the past two decades, the two rising capitalist states (Germany and Japan) have been attempting to establish independent access to sources of Middle East oil, bypassing the United States' postwar grip over the region through its control of a string of satellite nations from Iran to Saudi Arabia and the Persian Gulf states.

The most recent German and Japanese challenge to U.S. domination of Middle East oil prompted a swift response by the United States through massive U.S. military intervention in Saudi Arabia and the invasion of Iraq with the subsequent launching of the Persian Gulf War of 1991. The war was ostensibly launched to drive the Iraqi army out of Kuwait, but in fact was designed to punish Iraq for its role in cultivating close economic and geopolitical ties with United States' chief global economic rivals over access to and control of oil in the Middle East.[1]

Iran, Iraq, and Interimperialist Rivalry
in the Middle East

In the period from the early 1950s to the late 1970s—a period of uncontested U.S. supremacy in the Middle East—the United States firmly established itself in Iran and other countries of the Persian Gulf to control the flow of oil from the Middle East. By the 1970s, the United States became the chief importer of Iranian oil. Iranian exports to the United States, consisting primarily of crude oil, rose dramatically from $60 million in 1970 to $2.1 billion in 1974 to $4.3 billion in 1978, the final year of the shah's regime; in turn, imports from the United States rose sharply from $359 million in 1970 to $974 million in 1974 to $4.1 billion in 1978.[2] However, in the latter half of the 1970s interimperialist rivalries between the major capitalist powers began to reappear, as Japan, Germany, Britain, and other imperialist powers began to expand their trade relations with Iran.

Although the U.S. grip over Iran in the postwar period strengthened the shah's authoritarian rule and kept him in power for twenty-five years, it also prompted his regime to open up to other capitalist powers and to establish Iran as a regional subimperialist power in the Middle East.[3] Thus, in the latter half of the 1970s, Iranian exports (mainly oil) to Japan, Germany, and other European countries dramatically increased, while imports of consumer goods from these countries similarly increased.[4]

To counter these developments, Iraq—Iran's chief rival in the region—attracted Japan and a number of European countries, such as France and Italy, to meet their energy needs in exchange for imports of manufactured goods—a relationship Iraq sought to cultivate in building itself as an alternate regional power center in the Middle East. As a result, Iraqi exports to Japan, consisting primarily of oil, rose from $5 million in 1972 to $527 million in 1976 to $4 billion in 1980; to France, they increased from $268 million in 1972 to $1.5 billion in 1976 to $5.1 billion in 1980; and to Italy, they rose from $250 million in 1972 to $1.2 billion in 1976 to $2.6 billion in 1980.[5]

The overthrow of the shah's regime in 1979 and the accession to power of a new Islamic regime in Iran, followed by the war with Iraq, brought import-export trade between Iran and the United States to a virtual halt; but, despite these developments, Iran's trade with Japan, as well as with Germany and other European countries, continued to be on a strong footing throughout the 1980s. Thus while Iran's exports to the United States dropped from $4.3 billion in 1978 to $556 million in 1982 to a mere $2 million in 1990, exports to Japan made up bulk of Iran's total exports, amounting to $3.9 billion in 1978, $2.3 billion in 1982, and $3.2 billion in 1990.[6] Likewise, while imports from the United States declined from $4.1 billion in 1978 to $209 million in 1983 to $140 million in 1990, imports from Japan totaled $3 billion in 1978, $3.1 billion in 1983, and $1.8 billion in 1990; imports from Germany were also an important part of total Iranian imports, totaling $3.7 billion in 1978, $3.3 billion in 1983, and $2.8 billion in 1990.[7]

Clearly, over the past two decades, there has occurred a major shift in the export of Iranian oil away from the United States and toward Japan and various European countries. This is also evident in the source of Iranian imports. There has been a sharp drop in imports from the United States, but imports from Japan, Germany, and other European countries have substantially increased over the same period—indicating an apparent shift in patterns of political alliances manifested in import-export trade.

In Iraq, during the early 1980s, we see a similar pattern of trade relations with rival advanced capitalist countries. Japan, France, and Italy have been the prime recipients of Iraqi oil exports and, together with Germany, the major sources of Iraqi imports of manufactured goods. However, by the late 1980s, the United States began to tilt away from Iran and toward Iraq; it became the chief purchaser of Iraqi oil and the largest supplier of finished manufactured goods. Iraqi exports to the United States increased from $478 million in 1987 to $1.5 billion in 1988 to $2.3 billion in 1989 to $3 billion in 1990; imports of goods from the United States likewise rose from $752 million in 1987 to $1.3 billion in 1989, before dropping to $704 million in 1990.[8]

The rivalry between the chief imperialist powers vis-à-vis

access to and business with Iran and Iraq during the 1980s thus became intensified by the decade's end, and led to a regional power struggle between the two local centers. They vied for control over the Persian Gulf and for the best bargaining position vis-à-vis the rival imperialist powers. Iraq's invasion of Kuwait in August 1990, Bernard Headley points out, "had the potential to upset the balance of economic power in the Middle East and threatened the ability of Western (especially U.S. and British) powers to have a decisive influence over the terms and conditions of oil policy."[9] To counter such a possible development, Headley writes, the United States wanted to "use its military might to reassert Western control over the world's key resources and to reinforce U.S. strength in relation to its economic rivals."[10] "Iraq's invasion of Kuwait," he concludes, "provided an opportunity to implement this militaristic strategy for making sure the U.S. would be the world's undisputed superpower."[11]

The Gulf War of 1991

The United States went to war against Iraq in order to "liberate" Kuwait, to uphold freedom and the rule of law, and to take a stand against international aggression—so argued the U.S. administration, its Western allies, and its Arab collaborator regimes, which have brutally ruled the region for decades. In his State of the Union address, President Bush proclaimed: "What is at stake is . . . a new world order—where diverse nations are drawn together in common cause to achieve the universal aspirations of mankind: peace and security, freedom and the rule of law. . . . Saddam Hussein's unprovoked invasion . . . will not stand."[12]

If this could happen to the al-Sabah family in Kuwait, the argument went, it could also happen to the Saudi royal family, as well as the sultans and the emirs and their kind throughout the Gulf. This would mean that Saddam Hussein would next march down the Arabian Peninsula and eventually take over Saudi Arabia, and then the entire Gulf region, and finally the whole Middle East. But as Edward Greer points out,

The ground advanced to the American people to accede to attacking Iraq was that of the classical big lie: that the war to be waged was a collective and pre-emptive defense against a powerful regional criminal state, one with advanced means of mass destruction which it was in the process of deploying against world peace.

In retrospect, the ascribed reasons were false, and known to be such by the president. Iraq was not targeted because Hussein had launched an unprovoked military attack on a neighboring state which has major oil deposits. Saddam Hussein had already done precisely that to Iran a few years before, with active U.S. support.[13]

Greer goes on to point out:

Nor was Iraq targeted because it was defying United Nations resolutions condemning military aggression and occupation of another sovereign state or its territory. Neither the Turkish occupation of Cyprus, nor the Israeli occupation of the West Bank—both continuing to this day in contravention of similar resolutions—constituted a casus belli for the United States.[14]

Moreover, "nor was Iraq targeted for American military attack because Kuwait's medieval regime . . . embodied any political or cultural value dear to Americans."[15]

The massive intervention by the United States in the Gulf and the invasion of Iraq, despite proclamations to the contrary, was not for democracy and freedom, nor for "the rule of law"; not for "liberating" Kuwait, not for peace, not for security, and not for a "new" world order. Interestingly enough, it was not for the continued supply of oil to the United States either, for the United States neither depends on nor needs any significant amount of oil from the Middle East, as less than 10 percent of total U.S. oil consumption originates there. Other, more reliable and more secure sources, such as Mexico, Venezuela, and the North Sea, for example, can easily take up the slack. So, why then is the oil question raised at all?

What seems to be a complicated issue becomes clear and

revealing, once we discover that the oil controlled by the U.S. transnational oil companies in the Middle East is supplied mainly *not* to the United States, but to Germany and Japan—to fuel and thereby control the industrial life of the United States' chief rivals in the world economy: "Germany and Japan are rising economic powers, while Britain and the United States are declining. . . . As rising powers, Germany and Japan were not particularly threatened by Iraq's seizure of Kuwaiti resources. . . . Britain and the United States have had exactly the opposite reaction."[16]

As client states of the United States in the Gulf, Kuwait, Saudi Arabia, and the oil emirates play a key role in securing U.S. hegemony in the Middle East and its subsequent control of the flow of oil from this region. "The abolition of American suzerainty over oil-producing states of the Persian Gulf," writes Tom Mayer, "would threaten . . . the position of the United States relative to its principal commercial rivals."[17] Thus, "it is hardly surprising," Mayer adds, "that the United States should resort to war to repel a challenge to the imperial status quo. In the traditional fashion of declining economic powers (e.g., fourth-century imperial Rome, late fifteenth-century Spain, pre–First World War Britain), U.S. leaders are continually tempted to compensate for economic weakness with military force."[18]

The significance of control of sources of oil in the Middle East by the United States becomes evident as soon as one considers the alternative: how different the world might actually be if the oil fields now controlled by the U.S. oil companies were in fact controlled by those of Germany and Japan!

Post–Cold War Rivalries in the Political Economy of the Middle East

As the post–Cold War political economy of regional hostilities between the United States and the former Soviet Union have come to an end in the Middle East, this important region of the world has emerged as the arena for the unfolding rivalries between the major capitalist powers of the world over sources of the oil that is vital for their economies. Locked in interimperialist rivalries for control of raw materials, cheap labor, new markets, and higher rates of profit across the globe, the chief imperialist powers found in Iraq and Iran the potential for an alternate power center to control and regulate the flow of oil.

Clearly, both Germany and Japan have been searching for a surrogate power in the Gulf for over two decades. For a variety of reasons, including their financing of Iraq's decade-long war against Iran, Iraq was seen as the power that could secure for Japan and Germany a future foothold in the Middle East. Decline in influence of the United States in the region in post-shah and post-Saudi power politics and the rise of Germany and Japan through an expanding Iraqi hegemony over the Arabian Peninsula and the Gulf could thus secure for German and Japanese capital direct access to sources of oil in the Middle East, bypassing the traditionally dominant position of the U.S. oil companies in the region.

In an earlier period of British imperial control over the Middle East, U.S. encroachments on the region put it in direct rivalry with Britain over these territories, from Iran and Iraq to Jordan, Egypt, and down to the Arabian Peninsula including the entire Gulf region. Now, in the same strategic territories nearly a half century later, the same superpower rivals became involved in conflict once again, and for the very same reason—control of oil.

The disintegration of the Soviet Union as a military superpower, which during the postwar period played a key role in checking U.S. encroachments throughout the world, allowed the United States to intervene in the Gulf and succeed (at least for a while) in outmaneuvering its archrivals, Germany and Japan, denying them direct access to sources of oil essential to their economic independence and leading position in the world economy. Ironically, the outmaneuvered rivals—Germany and Japan—wound up paying a substantial portion of the cost of an operation designed to suppress them.[19] The cost to Iraq was enormous in both human and material terms: over one hundred thousand Iraqi soldiers and thousands of innocent civilians were killed in a high-tech massacre inflicted upon Iraq by the chief imperialist superpower, the United States.[20]

Now that the pre-August 1990 status quo has been secured in the Gulf and the United States is further entrenched in the Middle East, what are the lessons of the Gulf War for the future course of rivalry between the chief imperialist states in the world economy in the twenty-first century?

Having been denied direct access to Middle East oil, Germany, as the de facto leader of the European Community (EC), will play an increasingly central role within the EC and in relations with neighboring East European states. The relations will extend to a number of the former Soviet republics, notably Russia and Ukraine, just as Germany had a special relationship with the former Soviet Union through the infamous German-Soviet natural gas pipeline agreement in the late 1980s. In addition, linkage with Algeria via France (for natural gas), with Libya via Italy (for oil), and with Britain (for North Sea oil) are certainly within the realm of possibilities for the EC or Germany.

As the European economy continues to expand through increased commercial activity between member states, and as the EC becomes further consolidated through greater integration into a continental economic structure in which Germany continues to play a central role, the EC and its German nucleus will increasingly represent a viable challenge to U.S. power in the Middle East in the coming period.

Moreover, closer contact between Germany and Turkey, harkening back to a long-standing relationship between the two countries since the Ottoman period, may succeed in pulling Turkey away from the U.S. orbit in return for securing Turkish membership in the EC. This may also open access to the oil fields in eastern Turkey near the border with Iraq, and, through Turkey, extend Germany's influence to the latter's Central Asian ally, Azerbaijan, where Baku oil is exchanged for hard currency.

Whichever of these possibilities become a reality, it is clear that a rising economic power such as Germany cannot for long pretend to be challenging the United States, while all along continuing to be dependent on it for its most vital source of raw material, oil.

Japan has more limited but still quite viable access to sources of oil in its part of the world. The most likely source is China, where Japan has already invested more than $20 billion and enjoys a multiplicity of joint-venture benefits. China, as one of the world's largest producers of oil, would be more than eager to sell its excess capacity at levels below world market prices and still secure a steady source of guaranteed profits from its exports of this vital commodity to Japan and other rising capitalist economies in the region. Oil from Vietnam, Indonesia, and other Southeast Asian states, as well as from Siberia, could similarly fill an important part of Japanese demand and help Japan break loose from its dependence on the supply of Middle East oil controlled by the U.S. oil monopolies.

Now that the United States remains in firm control of the oil fields in the Middle East, while at the same time Europe is moving ahead with its full integration and Japan is continuing to expand its role and influence in the world economy, especially in the Pacific Rim, there is no doubt another clash of interests is bound to flare up—in Korea, Libya, the Philippines, Indonesia, the former Yugoslavia, or once again the Gulf?—as part of the long-standing rivalry between the chief protagonists of the world economy at the end of the twentieth and the early years of the twenty-first century.

Conclusion

For nearly two decades, since the overthrow of the shah's regime in Iran in 1979, Iran and Iraq have been at the center of rivalries between the chief imperialist states of the world capitalist system—the United States, Japan, Germany, and several other major European countries. The long and bloody war between Iran and Iraq during 1980–88 failed to fully resolve the power struggle between these rival regional powers in the Middle East, and the United States became the chief arbiter in determining the balance of forces between these two rising states by first siding with Iran, then with Iraq, and finally against both. Japan, Germany, France, Britain, and Italy have in turn built a trading partnership with Iran or Iraq, which are locked in a power struggle challenging the traditional dominance of this region by Egypt and Saudi Arabia under the tutelage of U.S. imperialism.

The Gulf War became a test case of territorial control within the larger context of Middle Eastern geopolitics. The direct intervention of the United States in its war against Iraq thus became the determinate response to the political turmoil that engulfed the region in the aftermath of the Cold War. The muscle flexed by the U.S. military machine in the Gulf was thus meant to send a clear message to its imperialist archrivals that the United States continues to play a key role in the political economy of the Middle East. This role, which had been a dominant one throughout the postwar period, has once again been reestablished in the post-Soviet, post–Cold War "new world order" that now defines the parameters of great power politics in the Middle East.

8

The Post–Cold War "New World Order" and the Prospect for Peace in the Middle East

The Gulf War of 1991 was an outcome of the end of the Cold War which set the stage for the emergence of the "New World Order"—one designed to replace the turmoil of the postwar years with a new, resurgent U.S. empire extending its reach to every corner of the world.[1] In the absence of a countervailing balance provided by the former USSR in international affairs, particularly in the Middle East, the United States became the sole arbiter of global conflicts, as well as the major force behind the Middle East peace process, which was driven by U.S. foreign policy interests.[2]

The question of Palestinian rights in the Occupied Territories, the domestic and foreign policies of the Israeli government, and the role of the Arab states in regional political alignments were all subsumed under U.S. strategic interests in the Middle East in the aftermath of the Gulf War. Unfortunately, the problems of the Middle East, which were local problems and required local solutions, became compounded when they began to increasingly reflect U.S. foreign policy interests in the region.

The U.S. approach to the political turmoil in the Middle East neglected the national and regional context of military conflict over the past several decades. This neglect stems from broader global geopolitical interests that were defined by the superpower rivalry of the postwar political economy fueled by the Cold War.[3] As a result, regional conflicts, driven by local, social, and political dynamics, came to be redefined by external imperialist intervention in the internal affairs of states in a typical neocolonial fashion. This was the case in Lebanon in the 1980s, where war and destruction in the aftermath of the civil war and the Israeli invasion had a great impact on the region's politics.[4] Another such area of conflict is Cyprus, which earlier erupted into war with the Turkish invasion of the island in 1974.[5]

The selective allowance by the imperialist states of a military solution to the long-standing political and territorial claims of local states led to the Iran-Iraq War of the 1980s, an action supported by the United States to destabilize the new Iranian regime.[6] The subsequent close relationship between the United States and Saddam Hussein in the war against Iran set the stage for the emergence of Iraq as a regional power—a development that allowed for the restructuring of the balance of forces in the Middle East more favorable to the United States.[7] Thus, following the "loss" of Iran in the aftermath of the Islamic Revolution, Iraq became the facilitator of U.S. strategic interests in the region until its invasion of Kuwait.

The increasing influence of Europe and Japan in the Middle East during the 1980s and the crisis in the former Soviet Union at the end of the decade gave the opening to the United States to make its move once again to recapture its declining position in the Middle East—a move that led to the massive intervention of the United States in the Persian Gulf and to the launching of the Gulf War of 1991.[8] The Gulf War was instrumental in reasserting the United States' traditional role and presence in the Middle East. It provided the basis for a resurgent U.S. empire in control of a region devastated by imperialism, war, and political turmoil.

An understanding of such developments in the broader context of the conflicts in the Middle East requires one to address the Palestinian question and the repression faced by the Kurds in Iraq and Turkey, as well as the reconstruction of Lebanon, the resolution of the conflict in Cyprus, and the control of political unrest stemming from the rise of Islamic fundamentalism in the region. These and other unresolved realities of life in the Middle East, which have once again taken center stage in political developments in the aftermath of the Gulf War, bring a new set of global contradictions to the fore and place the United States in the center of these conflicts, a situation that may generate yet unknown and unpredictable consequences with far greater impact on regional politics than those originally intended.

The Israeli invasion of Lebanon in 1982, for example, while intended to wipe out the strong Palestinian presence in that country following the Lebanese Civil War,[9] nonetheless led to a new set of contradictions; they went beyond the Palestinian question as such and extended to the nature of the anti-Israeli resistance, not only in Lebanon but also in the Occupied Territories and in Israel itself. Thus, the growth and expansion of the Islamic fundamentalist movement in the region became an unintended consequence of Israel's determination to end the power and influence of the PLO in Lebanon—a calculated move on Israel's part that backfired and made the situation worse. U.S. policy fostered Israel's vigilance in pursuing the PLO in southern Lebanon—and it later exacted from the United States a heavy price.[10]

The crisis in Lebanon during the 1980s led to a decade-long conflict that divided the country along ethno-religious lines. In the capital, Muslim West Beirut, seen as the hotbed of Islamic fundamentalism and the command post of the PLO, became counterposed to the "Christian" East, which enjoyed both Israeli and U.S. protection in the crisis years during and following the U.S. and Israeli presence in Beirut in the early 1980s.[11] A similar push from the south that shifted the political and military boundaries of engagement between the two sides came to effectively isolate the Muslim community in Lebanon, whose only recourse was to embrace the Syrian strategic foothold in the country.

The heavy Syrian presence in the North and the East to the coastal zone around Beirut and further south was aimed at neutralizing the Israeli forces, which were determined to hold on to southern Lebanon as a buffer zone and a staging ground for Israeli operations against the PLO.[12] The Israeli incursion into southern Lebanon and the isolation of West Beirut and other Lebanese towns populated by a predominantly Muslim population, however, more and more invited a radical, fundamentalist presence in Beirut and throughout the country that turned Lebanon into a hotbed of conflict and violence.[13]

The political forces intent on assuring their dominance in Lebanon thus increasingly resorted to religion as a mobilizing force to disarm the people and impose their will in national politics. Thus, the secular politics that characterized Lebanese political culture for decades slipped into factional strife. A multiplicity of new power centers were created within the segregated religious space, whose boundaries conveniently became the battle line that divided the city into rival political-military zones.

Beirut was transformed from a city of ethnic, national, religious, and political tolerance to a contested terrain of factional battles that brought destruction and death. The wounds of war and human suffering caused by organized force have turned the people of Lebanon into skeptics who doubt a reconciliation between the opposing sides will ever be possible. But, as economic reconstruction and political stability gradually foster the return to normalcy in Beirut in the coming years, Lebanon may once again enjoy peace that would contribute, in some small way, to the effort to end war and political turmoil in the Middle East.

The predicament of the Kurds in Iraq and Turkey and the denial of their right to national self-determination will continue to haunt the nations that suppress Kurdish demands to chart their national destiny.[14] The continued repression of the Kurdish people in Iraq and Turkey in the aftermath of the Gulf War will further strengthen their resolve to gain their freedom and determine their future in a free and independent Kurdistan. As one of the few remaining peoples in the world who have been denied a national homeland, the Kurds will no doubt continue their struggle and eventually succeed in taking their rightful place among the community of nation states in the not too distant future.

The prolonged struggle of the Palestinian people for national self-determination over the past several decades, however, attests to the protracted nature of the struggle for national autonomy and self-rule, which have been difficult to achieve.[15] The recent eruption of violence in Israel in response to the construction of new settlements in East Jerusalem has once again revealed the volatile nature of the peace process and has shown very clearly the Israeli intransigence over the future of the Occupied Territories. The new wave of unrest among Palestinians in Gaza and the West Bank reminds us once again that the final chapter on war and peace in this troubled region of the world has yet to be written.

Settlements will be built and dismantled, and sources of individual and state terrorism will be targeted and destroyed, yet new forms of violence will no doubt fan the flames of war and destruction. Ethnic strife, religious conflict, nationalist upheavals, and social revolution will continue to change the complex social, economic, and political landscape of this oil-rich region of the world, as will imperialism, war, and political turmoil.

It is not inevitable that a region, nation, or a people will be the permanent victims of social forces they have so far been unable to control, for often it is not they alone who chart the course of history. It is true that powerful forces have played a dominant role in determining the outcome of centuries of prolonged human misery, but many of these forces—whether empires or nation-states, exploiting classes or military dictatorships—have in the end been swept away into the dustbin of history, as the collective will of a determined people has prevailed over the forces of repression. Can one expect anything less (or hope for less than the possible) for the people of the Middle East?

NOTES

Chapter 1. The Impact of Western Imperialism on the Middle East

1. Roger Owen, *State, Power and Politics in the Making of the Modern Middle East* (London: Routledge, 1992), pp. 8–11.

2. "Imperialism" is the economic, political, and military domination of one nation by another for purposes of financial gain. Whereas historically imperialism can, in general, be defined in these terms (e.g., as it applies to the Ottoman Empire), modern imperialism is defined as the monopoly stage of capitalism that spans the period from the late nineteenth through the twentieth century to the present. Like colonialism, modern-day imperialism involves the exploitation and/or oppression of a nation and its population, land, and resources for purposes of profit, but unlike colonialism, which entails direct political/military rule, contemporary imperialism connotes control and domination of a nation by indirect means through the instrumentality of a variety of global imperial institutions.

3. E. M. Earle, *Turkey, The Great Powers, and the Bagdad Railway: A Study in Imperialism* (New York: Russell & Russell, 1966), p. 13; T. Cavdar, "Cumhuriyet Devri Baslarken Türkiye Ekonomisi" (The Turkish economy at the beginning of the republican era), in *Türkiye Ekonomisinin 50 Yili Semineri* (Bursa: I. ve T. I. Akademisi, 1973), p. 62.

4. O. C. Sarc, "Ottoman Industrial Policy, 1840–1914," in *The Economic History of the Middle East, 1800–1914*, ed. Charles Issawi (Chicago: University of Chicago Press, 1966), pp. 52–55.

5. Resat Kasaba, *The Ottoman Empire and the World Economy—The*

Nineteenth Century (Albany: State University of New York Press, 1988), chaps. 2 and 3. However, this did not mean a complete blockage of capitalist development in Turkey, but a temporary halt in the development of a Turkish national industrial bourgeoisie. The limited capitalism that did develop in the empire from the mid-nineteenth to the beginning of the twentieth centuries was effected through the intermediary of the Ottoman minority commercial bourgeoisie. See Hüseyin Ramazanoglu, "A Political Analysis of the Emergence of Turkish Capitalism, 1839–1950," in *Turkey in the World Capitalist System*, ed. H. Ramazanoglu (Aldershot, U.K.: Gower, 1985), pp. 49–54.

6. Owen, *State, Power and Politics in the Making of the Modern Middle East*, pp. 8–11.

7. Ibid., p. 9.

8. Ibid., pp. 10–11.

9. T. Cavdar, *Osmanlilarin Yari Sömürge Olusu* (The semicolonization of the Ottomans) (Istanbul: Ant Yayinlari, 1970).

10. Joe Stork, *Middle East Oil and the Energy Crisis* (New York: Monthly Review Press, 1975), p. 7.

11. Ibid., p. 8.

12. D. C. Blaisdell, *European Financial Control in the Ottoman Empire* (New York: Columbia University Press, 1929).

13. Alain Gresh and Dominique Vidal, eds., *An A to Z of the Middle East* (London: Zed Books, 1990), p. 141.

14. Earle, *Turkey, the Great Powers, and the Bagdad Railway*, pp. 4–5.

15. Ibid., pp. 7–8.

16. Ibid., p. 8.

17. Ibid., p. 15.

18. Ibid., pp. 15, 17.

19. Ibid., p. 36.

20. Ibid. Earle goes on to point out: "The London *Times* of October 28, 1898, contained a significant review of the status of German enterprise in the Ottoman Empire during the decade immediately preceding. Whereas ten years before, the finance and trade of [Ottoman] Turkey were practically monopolized by France and Great Britain, the Germans were now by far the most active group in Constantinople and in Asia Minor." Ibid., p. 37. More specifically, "The Krupp-owned Germania Shipbuilding Company was furnishing torpedoes to the Turkish navy; Ludwig Loewe and Company, of Berlin, was equipping the Sultan's military machine with small arms; Krupp, of Essen, was sharing with Armstrong the orders for artillery. . . . In 1899 a group of German financiers founded the *Deutsche Palästina Bank*, which pro-

ceeded to establish branches at Beirut, Damascus, Gaza, Haifa, Jaffa, Jerusalem, Nablus, Nazareth, and Tripoli-in-Syria." Ibid.

21. Ibid.

22. Ibid., p. 341.

23. Ibid., p. 343.

24. Ibid.

25. Gresh and Vidal, eds., *An A to Z of the Middle East*, p. 52.

26. Stork, *Middle East Oil and the Energy Crisis*, p. 14.

27. Daniel Yergin, *The Prize: The Epic Quest for Oil, Money, and Power* (New York: Simon & Schuster, 1991).

28. William Stivers, *Supremacy and Oil: Iraq, Turkey, and the Anglo-American World Order, 1918–1930* (Ithaca: Cornell University Press, 1982), p. 15.

29. Gresh and Vidal, eds. *An A to Z of the Middle East*, p. 54.

30. By 1948, the United States came to control more than half of Middle East oil production.

31. Oil exports have accounted for more than 90 percent of total exports of Iran and Iraq during the past two decades. In 1990, oil exports accounted for 92 percent of Iran's total exports and 99.4 percent of Iraq's total exports. See Organization of Petroleum Exporting Countries, *OPEC Annual Statistical Bulletin, 1991* (Vienna: OPEC, 1992), p. 8.

32. Farideh Farhi, "Class Struggles, the State, and Revolution in Iran," in *Power and Stability in the Middle East*, ed. Berch Berberoglu (London: Zed Books, 1989); Cyrus Bina and Hamid Zangeneh, eds., *Modern Capitalism and Islamic Ideology in Iran* (New York: St. Martin's Press, 1992).

33. Haim Bresheeth and Nira Yuval-Davis, introduction to *The Gulf War and the New World Order*, ed. Haim Bresheeth and Nira Yuval-Davis (London: Zed Books, 1991), p. 1.

34. Ibid.

35. Ibid.

Chapter 2. Nationalism, Ethnic Conflict, and Political Turmoil in the Middle East in the Early Twentieth Century

1. "Nationalism" is defined here as an ideology that upholds adherence to the nation above all other group identity, such as social class or religion. It promotes the interests of one nation (or ethnic group) over all others and is normally the ideology of the national and/or petty bourgeoisie, though sometimes it is used by other classes to advance a particular class interest. For further discussion on the nature

and dynamics of nationalism, see Berch Berberoglu, *Class, State and Nation: The Class Nature of Nationalism and Ethnic Conflict* (Westport, Conn.: Greenwood Press, 2000), chaps. 1 and 2.

2. Charles Issawi, *The Economic History of Turkey, 1800–1914* (Chicago: University of Chicago Press, 1980), p. 54.

3. Hrachya Adjarian, "Hayots dere Osmanian Kaysrutyean medj," in *Banber Erevani Hamalsarani* (Yerevan, Armenia: Yerevan State University Press, 1967), cited in ibid., p. 62. See also S. Shaw, "The Ottoman Census System and Population, 1831–1914," *International Journal of Middle East Studies* 9 (1978): 332; Kemal H. Karpat, *Ottoman Population, 1830–1914: Demographic and Social Characteristics* (Madison: University of Wisconsin Press, 1985), pp. 51–55; and idem, "Ottoman Population Records and the Census of 1881/82–1893," *International Journal of Middle East Studies* 9 (1978): 254.

4. Alphons Sussnitski, "Die wirtschaftliche Lage der Juden in Konstantinopel," *Allgemeine Zeitung des Judentums* (Berlin), 8, 12, and 19 January 1912, in Issawi, *Economic History of Turkey*, p. 70.

5. Charles Issawi, *The Economic History of the Middle East and North Africa* (New York: Columbia University Press, 1982), p. 6.

6. Ibid.

7. Ibid., pp. 89–90.

8. Halit Ziya Usakligil, *Kirk Yil*, 5 vols. (Istanbul: Matbaacilik ve Nesriyat, 1936), excerpted in Issawi, *Economic History of Turkey*, pp. 72–73.

9. Vartan Artinian, "A Study of the Historical Development of the Armenian Constitutional System in the Ottoman Empire" (Ph.D. diss., Brandeis University, 1970); and idem, "The Formation of Catholic and Protestant Millets in the Ottoman Empire," *Armenian Review* 28 (Spring 1975): 3–15.

10. Artinian, "Armenian Constitutional System." See also Karpat, *Ottoman Population, 1830–1914*, pp. 51–55; and Justin McCarthy, *Muslims and Minorities* (New York: New York University Press, 1983), pp. 47–88 for various contradictory estimates of the Armenian population by the Armenian Patriarchate and the Ottoman government, as well as by independent European sources.

11. Christopher J. Walker, *Armenia: The Survival of a Nation* (New York: St. Martin's Press, 1980), pp. 94–95.

12. Among the more important trades in which Armenian craftsmen were prominent were: jewelry, textiles, work with gold, silver, and copper, and shoemaking. See L. Arpee, *The Armenian Awakening, 1820–1860* (Chicago: University of Chicago Press, 1909); and Grigor

Zohrap, *La Question Armenienne à la Lumière des Documents* (Paris: A. Challamel, 1913). See also Walker, *Armenia*, pp. 94–98.

13. *Ermeni* means "Armenian" in Turkish. The *Ermeni millet* refers to the Armenian national/ethnic community.

14. Louise Nalbandian, *The Armenian Revolutionary Movement* (Berkeley: University of California Press, 1967), p. 43.

15. Ibid.

16. As Artinian points out, "By the middle of the nineteenth century there were over thirty Armenian commercial firms in London and Manchester with their headquarters located either in Smyrna [Izmir] or Istanbul." Artinian, "Armenian Constitutional System," p. 7. See also Walker, *Armenia*.

17. Issawi, *Economic History of Turkey*, p. 62.

18. Walker, *Armenia*, p. 97. This was also the case in the territories adjacent to Ottoman Turkey, such as in Russian Transcaucasia. As Walker points out, "The Armenian bourgeoisie... became the dominant commercial class in Tiflis, Baku and the other cities of Transcaucasia. By 1876 two thirds of the merchants in Tiflis were Armenian, and four out of the six banks were controlled by Armenians; in Baku, by the last decade of the century, Armenians controlled more than half the oil wells." Walker, *Armenia*, pp. 60–61.

19. Adjarian, "Hayots dere Osmanian Kaysrutyean medj," in Issawi, *Economic History of Turkey*, p. 62. However, Hagop Barsoumian points out that, despite their enormous wealth and power within the Armenian community, the *amiras* had virtually no political power within the Ottoman state. Hagop Barsoumian, "The Dual Role of the Armenian Amira Class within the Ottoman Government and the Armenian Millet (1750–1850)," in *Christians and Jews in the Ottoman Empire*, ed. Benjamin Braude and Bernard Lewis (New York: Holmes & Meier, 1982), pp. 176–77. See also Üner A. Turgay, "Trade and Merchants in Nineteenth-Century Trabzon: Elements of Ethnic Conflict," in *Christians and Jews in the Ottoman Empire*, ed. Braude and Lewis, p. 305.

20. Mesrob K. Krikorian, *Armenians in the Service of the Ottoman Empire, 1860–1908* (London: Routledge & Kegan Paul, 1977).

21. Adjarian, "Hayots dere Osmanian Kaysrutyean medj," p. 63.

22. Sir Charles Eliot, *Turkey in Europe* (New York: Barnes & Noble, 1965), p. 153; Turgay, "Trade and Merchants in Nineteenth-Century Trabzon," p. 305.

23. Cited in Issawi, *Economic History of Turkey*, p. 65.

24. M. S. Lazarev, *Kurdistan i Kurdskaia Problema* (Moscow: Nauka, 1964) in ibid., p. 67. Another (Austrian) source, which provides more

details on the number of Armenians in the Sivas province engaged in various businesses, confirms this, while being slightly at variance with Lazarev's figures in two instances. Namely, number of Armenian large importers is reported here as being 141 (instead of 125) out of 166, and Armenian owners of industrial enterprises 127 (instead of 130) out of 150. See Freiherrn M. Kapri, *Die Historische und kulturelle Bedeutung des armenischen Volkes* (Wien: Mechitharisten-Buchdruckerei, 1913), pp. 65–67.

25. Cited in Issawi, *Economic History of Turkey*, p. 56.

26. W. M. Ramsay, *Impressions of Turkey* (London: Hodder & Stoughton, 1897), pp. 130–31.

27. Issawi, *Economic History of Turkey*, p. 56.

28. Robert Melson, "A Theoretical Inquiry into the Armenian Massacres of 1894–1896," *Comparative Studies in Society and History* 24, no. 3 (July 1982): 481–509.

29. According to W. L. Langer, "blood was shed in the capital [Istanbul] itself; in the provinces there were massacres at Trebizond and many other places. . . . It was perfectly obvious that the Sultan [Abdul Hamid] was determined to end the Armenian question by exterminating the Armenians." William L. Langer, *The Diplomacy of Imperialism, 1890–1902*, vol. 1 (New York: Alfred A. Knopf, 1935), p. 203.

30. For a documentation of the Armenian genocide and the extent of the massacres, see: *Christians and Jews in the Ottoman Empire*, ed. Braude and Lewis; Vahakn N. Dadrian, "Genocide as a Problem of National and International Law: The World War I Armenian Case and Its Contemporary Legal Ramifications," *Yale Journal of International Law* 14, no. 2 (Summer 1989): 272; Gerard Chaliand and Yves Ternon, *The Armenians: From Genocide to Resistance* (London: Zed Books, 1983); and Permanent Peoples' Tribunal, *A Crime of Silence: The Armenian Genocide* (London: Zed Books, 1985).

31. The events that sparked the massacres of 1894–96 include the uprising of Armenians in Talori; in the Vilayet of Bitlis, where Ottoman troops were sent to quell the revolt; a mass demonstration in August 1895; and the armed occupation of the Ottoman Bank by Armenian revolutionaries in September 1896. See Melson, "A Theoretical Inquiry into the Armenian Massacres of 1894–1896," pp. 481–509.

32. Paul Saba, "The Armenian National Question," in *Power and Stability in the Middle East*, ed. Berberoglu, p. 188. On this point, see also Akaby Nassibian, *Britain and the Armenian Question, 1915–1923* (New York: St. Martin's Press, 1984), p. 26.

33. Saba, "The Armenian National Question," p. 189.

34. Ibid.

35. Ibid.

36. Ibid.
37. Ibid., pp. 189–90.
38. Ibid., p. 190.
39. For an extended bibliographic compilation of historical sources on the Armenian genocide, see Richard G. Hovannisian, *The Armenian Holocaust* (Cambridge, Mass.: Armenian Heritage Press, 1978) and Vahakn N. Dadrian, "The Naim-Andonian Documents on the World War I Destruction of Ottoman Armenians: The Anatomy of a Genocide," *International Journal of Middle East Studies* 18 (1986): 311–60. See also Chaliand and Ternon, *Armenians;* Permanent Peoples' Tribunal, *Crime of Silence;* and Vahakn N. Dadrian, *The History of the Armenian Genocide* (Providence, R.I.: Berghahn Books, 1995).

40. Walker, *Armenia*, p. 230. Paul Saba points out that in terms of the very survival of Armenians as an ethnic group, "the year 1915 was one of disaster for the Armenians. Before the war it has been estimated that there were between 1,500,000 and 2,000,000 Armenians in the Ottoman Empire. By 1916, some 250,000 had managed to flee to Russia and escape the carnage. Another 1,000,000 were killed, half of them women and children. Of the approximately 600,000 survivors, about 200,000 were forcibly converted to Islam. The remaining 400,000, mostly in refugee and concentration camps, suffered a wretched existence. Some 50,000 to 100,000 of these were killed during the Turkish invasion of the Caucasus in May–September 1918, while approximately another 250,000 were murdered in 1919–1923 during post-war attempts by survivors to return to their homes." Saba, "The Armenian National Question," pp. 190–91.

41. In April 1995, the eightieth anniversary of the Armenian genocide was commemorated at the International Conference on Problems of Genocide, which took place at the National Academy of Sciences in Yerevan, Armenia. An abbreviated version of this chapter was presented there. The conference proceedings were subsequently published by the Zoryan Institute under the title *Problems of Genocide* (Toronto: Zoryan Institute of Canada, 1997).

Chapter 3. Imperialism and the Resurgence of
Nationalism in the Middle East: Turkey and Egypt

1. Bernard Lewis, *The Emergence of Modern Turkey*, 2d ed. (New York: Oxford University Press, 1969), pp. 210–38.

2. Feroz Ahmad, *The Young Turks: The Committee of Union and Progress in Turkish Politics, 1908–1914* (London: Oxford University Press, 1969); E. E. Ramsaur, *The Young Turks: Prelude to the Revolution of 1908* (Beirut: Khayat, 1965).

3. Lewis, *Emergence of Modern Turkey*, pp. 239–40.

4. Ibid., p. 240.

5. Ibid., p. 241.

6. Ibid.

7. Ibid.

8. "Comprador bourgeoisie" consists of that segment of the local capitalist class that is engaged in import-export trade and other commercial activities directly tied to the imperial centers.

9. Berch Berberoglu, *Turkey in Crisis: From State Capitalism to Neo-Colonialism* (London: Zed Press, 1982), p. 9.

10. Ibid.

11. Ibid., p. 11. See also Hüseyin Ramazanoglu, "A Political Analysis of the Emergence of Turkish Capitalism, 1839–1950," in *Turkey in the World Capitalist System*, ed. Ramazanoglu, pp. 54–66.

"Petty bourgeoisie" is defined here as those who own and/or control means of production, but employ no wage laborers. The self-employed (or small shopkeepers, artisans, and landed peasants) have traditionally been viewed as constituting the core of this class. The petty bourgeoisie also includes professionals, middle-level government bureaucrats, and other intermediate sectors of society in general. As an intermediate class, the petty bourgeoisie is caught between the dominant ruling class(es) and the working class, with both of which it has certain shared characteristics. Like the big bourgeoisie and landlords, it owns or controls means of production, and, like the working class, it is directly engaged in the production process, hence it provides its own labor power. Thus, the petty bourgeoisie is neither an exploiting class nor an exploited one. While members of this class aspire to become big capitalists, their immediate interests center around the safeguarding of their position as small independent producers or professionals. When we refer to the military and civilian sectors of the state bureaucracy as petty bourgeois, it is not because the bureaucracy in itself occupies an intermediate position within class society, but because in most postcolonial or neocolonial Third World societies officers in both of these sectors (especially junior officers in the army, who are often the main leaders inciting anti-imperialist military coups) are drawn from the ranks of the petty bourgeoisie.

12. Turgut Taylan, "Capital and the State in Contemporary Turkey," *Khamsin*, no. 11 (1984): 7–8.

13. Çaglar Keyder, *State and Class in Turkey* (London: Verso, 1987), pp. 91–115.

14. Ibid.

15. "National industrial bourgeoisie," or simply "national bourgeoisie," is composed of that segment of the local capitalist class that owns/controls the means of industrial production. While the comprador bourgeoisie is mainly concentrated in import-export trade and is directly tied to the imperial centers, the national bourgeoisie has interests that are local and thus nationally based. The "nationalism" of local industrial capitalists is the result of their concern to safeguard and protect property in the means of production that is located within the confines of their own national territory.

16. H. Derin, *Türkiye'de Devletçilik* (Statism in Turkey) (Istanbul: Cituri Biraderler, 1940), p. 83. Parallel to the process of development and expansion of native industry, a number of important steps were also taken by the state in this period to accelerate the process of capital accumulation in the countryside. Among these were the abolition of the *ösür* (tithe tax) in 1925 and the distribution of land to landless peasants through laws passed in 1927 and 1929. As a result, by 1934 a total of 7,114,315 *dönüm* (or 17,785,787 acres) of land were distributed to those without land. See S. Aksoy, *Türkiye'de Toprak Meselesi* (The land question in Turkey), (Istanbul: Gerçek Yayinevi, 1971), pp. 52–67.

17. "State capitalism" in the Third World is a type of regime that challenges the neocolonial social order and takes action against foreign capital in order to facilitate national capitalist accumulation, because class forces sympathetic to national capitalist development have captured state power and have replaced the rule of the old neocolonial power bloc. We contend that, under state capitalism in the Third World the state is dominated and controlled by the petty bourgeoisie. The latter is led by the military and civilian sectors of the state bureaucracy.

18. Berberoglu, *Turkey in Crisis*, pp. 34–65.

19. Dogu Ergil, "From Empire to Dependence: The Evolution of Turkish Underdevelopment" (Ph.D. diss., State University of New York at Binghamton, 1975).

20. Ramazanoglu, *Turkey in the World Capitalist System*, pp. 69–70.

21. Taylan, "Capital and the State in Contemporary Turkey," pp. 10–11.

22. Berberoglu, *Turkey in Crisis*, pp. 128–32.

23. Richard C. Whiting, "The Suez Canal and the British Economy 1918–1960," in *Imperialism and Nationalism in the Middle East*, ed. Keith M. Wilson (London: Mansell, 1983), p. 84.

24. Ibid., p. 79.

25. Ibid., p. 76.

26. Kirk J. Beattie, *Egypt During the Nasser Years* (Boulder, Colo.: Westview Press, 1994), pp. 66–67.

27. Peter Mansfield, *Nasser's Egypt* (Baltimore, Md.: Penguin, 1965), p. 43.

28. Samir Amin, *The Arab Nation: Nationalism and Class Struggles* (London: Zed Press, 1978).

29. Ahmad N. Azim, "Egypt: The Origins and Development of a Neo-colonial State," in *Power and Stability in the Middle East*, ed. Berberoglu, p. 4.

30. Ibid.

31. Mansfield, *Nasser's Egypt*, p. 135.

32. Ibid., pp. 4–5.

33. Mahmoud Hussain, *Class Conflict in Egypt, 1945–1970* (New York: Monthly Review Press, 1973). Hussain, in fact, goes a step further in tracing the role of the state (and that of petty-bourgeois state bureaucrats) in the accumulation process and argues that by virtue of their strategic position in control of state property, state officials became transformed into a new dominant class—a "state bourgeoisie." It had interests that were complementary with those of the ruling classes, since it directly benefited from (state-directed) capitalist development. See ibid., pp. 104–9.

34. Mark Cooper, "Egyptian State Capitalism in Crisis," in *The Middle East*, ed. Talal Asad and Roger Owen (New York: Monthly Review Press, 1983). See also Joel Beinin, "Egypt's Transition Under Nasser," *MERIP Reports* 107 (July/August 1982).

35. Azim, "Egypt: The Origins and Development of a Neo-colonial State," p. 11.

36. Ibid. See also Ghali Shoukri, *Egypt: Portrait of a President* (London: Zed Press, 1981).

37. Jim Paul, "Foreign Investment in Egypt," *MERIP Reports* 107 (July/August 1982): 17. Foreign investment in Egypt during this period was concentrated most heavily in petroleum, banking, chemicals, pharmaceuticals, and other branches of manufacturing industry, especially electronics and transportation equipment.

38. See Charles Tripp and Roger Owens, eds., *Egypt Under Mubarak* (London: Routledge, 1989).

Chapter 4. Imperialism and the Resurgence of Nationalism in the Middle East: Syria and Iraq

1. A. H. Hourani, *Syria and Lebanon: A Political Essay* (London: RIIA, 1946).

2. Derek Hopwood, *Syria, 1945–1986: Politics and Society* (London: Unwin Hyman, 1988), pp. 22–24.

3. Nikolaos Van Dam, *The Struggle for Power in Syria* (New York: St. Martin's Press, 1979), p. 18.

4. Philip S. Khoury, *Syria and the French Mandate: The Politics of Arab Nationalism, 1920–1945* (Princeton: Princeton University Press, 1987), pp. 615–18.

5. Tabitha Petran, *Syria* (New York: Praeger, 1972), p. 96.

6. Ibid.

7. Ibid.

8. Ibid., p. 101.

9. Ibid.

10. Ibid., p. 103.

11. Ibid., pp. 106–47.

12. Hopwood, *Syria, 1945–1986*, p. 40.

13. Ibid., p. 41.

14. Ibid.

15. Ibid.

16. Ibid., p. 42.

17. David Roberts, *The Ba'th and the Creation of Modern Syria* (New York: St. Martin's Press, 1987), pp. 54–58.

18. Fred H. Lawson, "Class Politics and State Power in Ba'thi Syria," in *Power and Stability in the Middle East*, ed. Berberoglu, pp. 20–21.

19. An initial coup led by General al-Asad in 1969 met with strong opposition from politicians and organized groups. This prompted Asad to make a stronger move with a second coup in 1970, which effectively secured for him firm control over the state apparatus.

20. Petran, *Syria*, pp. 251–52.

21. Elizabeth Longuenesse, "The Class Nature of the State in Syria" *MERIP Reports* 9, no. 4 (May 1979).

22. William Stivers, *Supremacy and Oil: Iraq, Turkey, and the Anglo-American World Order, 1918–1930* (Ithaca: Cornell University Press, 1982).

23. Kedourie, "Great Britain, the Other Powers, and the Middle East Before and After World War I," in *Great Powers in the Middle East, 1919–1939*, ed. Uriel Dann (New York: Holmes & Meier, 1988), pp. 8–9.

24. Joe Stork, "Class, State and Politics in Iraq," in *Power and Stability in the Middle East*, ed. Berberoglu, p. 31.

25. Ibid., pp. 31–32.

26. Ibid., p. 32.

27. Hanna Batatu, *The Old Social Classes and the Revolutionary Movements in Iraq* (Princeton: Princeton University Press, 1978).

28. Marion Farouk-Sluglett and Peter Sluglett, "The Social Classes and the Origins of the Revolution," in *The Iraqi Revolution of 1958*, ed.

Robert A. Fernea and Wm. Roger Louis (New York: I. B. Tauris, 1991), pp. 126–27.

29. Ibid., p. 127.

30. Ibid.

31. Fahim Qubain, *The Reconstruction of Iraq, 1950–57* (New York: Praeger, 1958); E. A. Finch, "Social Effects of the Oil Industry in Iraq," *International Labour Review*, March 1957; and Kathleen Langley, *The Industrialization of Iraq* (Cambridge: Harvard University Press, 1961).

32. Batatu, *The Old Social Classes and the Revolutionary Movements in Iraq.*

33. Marion Farouk-Sluglett and Peter Sluglett, *Iraq Since 1958: From Revolution to Dictatorship* (London: KPI, 1987), pp. 47–55.

34. Tim Niblock, introduction to *Iraq: The Contemporary State*, ed. Tim Niblock (New York: St. Martin's Press, 1982), p. 4.

35. Majid Khadduri, *Republican Iraq* (London: Oxford University Press, 1969).

36. Fran Hazelton, "Iraq to 1963," in *Saddam's Iraq: Revolution or Reaction?* ed. Committee Against Repression and for Democratic Rights in Iraq (CARDRI) (London: Zed Books, 1989), pp. 26–27.

37. U. Zaher, "Political Developments in Iraq 1963–1980," in *Saddam's Iraq: Revolution or Reaction?*, ed. CARDRI, p. 30.

38. Ibid., p. 31.

39. Ibid., pp. 31–32.

40. Abbas Alnasrawi, "Economic Devastation, Underdevelopment and Outlook," in *Iraq Since the Gulf War*, ed. Fran Hazelton (London: Zed Books, 1994), p. 74.

41. Ibid.

42. Ibid.

Chapter 5. The National Question in the Middle East: The Palestinian and Kurdish Struggles for National Self-Determination

1. Edward W. Said, *The Politics of Dispossession: The Struggle for Palestinian Self-Determination, 1969–1994* (New York: Pantheon, 1994).

2. Gordon Welty, "Palestinian Nationalism and the Struggle for National Self-Determination," in *The National Question: Nationalism, Ethnic Conflict and Self-Determination in the Twentieth Century*, ed. Berch Berberoglu (Philadelphia: Temple University Press, 1995), p. 16.

3. Ibid., p. 17.

4. Baruch Kimmerling and Joel S. Migdal, *Palestinians: The Making of a People* (New York: The Free Press, 1993), pp. 130–31.

5. Pamela Ann Smith, "Palestine and the Palestinians," in *Power and Stability in the Middle East*, ed. Berberoglu, p. 157.

6. Ibid., pp. 157, 159.

7. Estimates of the total number of Palestinians in the diaspora vary, but there is a general consensus among authors that it is somewhere around 4.5 to 5 million.

8. Smith, "Palestine and the Palestinians," p. 159.

9. Ibid., p. 160.

10. Government of Palestine, *A Survey of Palestine*, 2 vols. (Jerusalem: Government of Palestine, 1946), 2:569, cited in Smith, "Palestine and the Palestinians," p. 171.

11. Smith, "Palestine and the Palestinians," p. 160.

12. Ibid. See also J. C. Hurewitz, *The Struggle for Palestine* (New York: Greenwood Press, 1968).

13. David McDowall, *The Palestinians: The Road to Nationhood* (London: Minority Rights Group, 1995).

14. Welty, "Palestinian Nationalism," p. 18.

15. Ibid.

16. Ibid., p. 19. See also Salim Tamari, "Factionalism and Class Formation in Recent Palestinian History," in *Studies in the Economic and Social History of Palestine in the Nineteenth and Twentieth Centuries*, ed. Roger Owen (London: Macmillan, 1982), chap. 3.

17. See Kimmerling and Migdal, *Palestinians*, pp. 96–123.

18. Ibid., p. 96.

19. Ibid., pp. 96–97.

20. Welty, "Palestinian Nationalism," p. 21.

21. Ibid., p. 22.

22. Ibid. See also Nur Masalha, *Expulsion of the Palestinians* (Washington, D.C.: Institute for Palestine Studies, 1992).

23. Welty, "Palestinian Nationalism," p. 22.

24. Said, *Politics of Dispossession*.

25. Helena Cobban, *The Palestinian Liberation Organization* (Cambridge: Cambridge University Press, 1984). See also Alain Gresh, *The PLO: The Struggle Within* (London: Zed Books, 1985).

26. Rosemary Sayigh, *Palestinians: From Peasants to Revolutionaries* (London: Zed Press, 1979), pp. 152–54.

27. Gerard Chaliand, *The Palestinian Resistance* (Baltimore, Md.: Penguin, 1972), pp. 60–61.

28. Welty, "Palestinian Nationalism," p. 24.

29. Ibid., p. 25.

30. Chaliand, *Palestinian Resistance*, pp. 84–129.

31. See John Cooley, *Green March, Black September* (London: Frank Cass, 1973), pp. 109–22.

32. James Reilly, "Israel in Lebanon, 1975–82," *MERIP Reports* 12, nos. 6–7 (September–October 1982).

33. See Samih Farsoun, "Israel's Goal of Destroying the PLO is Not Achievable," *Journal of Palestine Studies* 11, no. 4 (1982).

34. Zachary Lockman and Joel Beinin, *Intifada: The Palestinian Uprising Against Israeli Occupation* (Boston: South End Press, 1989).

35. Martin Van Bruinessen, *Agha, Shaikh and State: The Social and Political Structures of Kurdistan* (London: Zed Books, 1992), pp. 133–95. See also Abdul Rahman Ghassemlou, *Kurdistan and the Kurds* (London: Collets Holdings, 1965).

36. Ferhad Ibrahim, "The Kurdish National Movement and the Struggle for National Autonomy," in *National Question*, ed. Berberoglu, pp. 38–39.

37. Ibid., p. 39.

38. Ibid., p. 36. For slightly different estimates of the total Kurdish population, and of Kurds in the various countries in which they are found, see David McDowall, *A Modern History of the Kurds* (London: I. B. Tauris, 1996), pp. 3–4.

39. Bruinessen, *Agha, Shaikh and State*, p. 51.

40. Ibid., p. 50.

41. Gerard Chaliand, *The Kurdish Tragedy* (London: Zed Books, 1994), p. 19.

42. Bruinessen, *Agha, Shaikh and State*, p. 50.

43. Ibrahim, "The Kurdish National Movement," p. 37.

44. Chaliand, *Kurdish Tragedy*, pp. 14–15.

45. Kendal, "Kurdistan in Turkey," in *People Without a Country*, ed. Gerard Chaliand (London: Zed Press, 1980), p. 89.

46. Ibid., pp. 83–87.

47. Bruinessen, *Agha, Shaikh and the State*, pp. 21–22.

48. Ibid., p. 37.

49. Ibrahim, "The Kurdish National Movement," pp. 39–40.

50. See the text of relevant sections of the Treaty of Sevres (Articles 62–64) in McDowall, *Modern History of the Kurds*, pp. 450–51.

51. See Ismet Sheriff Vanly, *Survey of the National Question of Turkish Kurdistan with Historical Background* (Zurich: Hevra, 1971).

52. Ibrahim, "The Kurdish National Movement," p. 40.

53. Kendal, "Kurdistan in Turkey," p. 61.

54. See Edmund Ghareeb, *The Kurdish Question in Iraq* (Syracuse, N.Y.: Syracuse University Press, 1981). See also the essays by Ghassemlou, Kendal, Nazdar, and Vanly in Chaliand, *People Without a Country.*

55. William Eagleton Jr., *The Kurdish Republic of 1946* (London: Oxford University Press, 1963).

56. Ibrahim, "The Kurdish National Movement," p. 41.

57. Bruinessen, *Agha, Shaikh and State*, p. 33.

58. Ibid., p. 42.

59. David McDowall, *The Kurds: A Nation Denied* (London: Minority Rights Group, 1992), pp. 44–47.

60. Ibid., p. 45.

61. Ibrahim, "The Kurdish National Movement," pp. 53–54.

62. Ibid., p. 51.

63. McDowall, *Kurds*, p. 52.

64. Martin van Bruinessen, "Kurdish Society, Ethnicity, Nationalism and Refugee Problems," in *The Kurds: A Contemporary Overview,* ed. Philip G. Kreyenbroek and Stefan Sperl (London: Routledge, 1992), p. 59.

65. Ibrahim, "The Kurdish National Movement," p. 52.

66. Ibid., p. 44.

67. Bruinessen, *Agha, Shaikh and State*, pp. 36–37.

68. "It remains unclear," writes Bruinessen, "to what extent they [the Iraqi KDP] were forced to join the fight against the Iranian Kurds or did so voluntarily. Clearly the Iraqi KDP was highly suspicious of its sister party's contacts with Baghdad." Ibid., p. 39.

69. Ibid., p. 43.

70. Ibid., p. 44.

Chapter 6. The Arab-Israeli Conflict: War and Political Turmoil in the Middle East

1. F. Trablusi, "The Palestine Problem: Zionism and Imperialism in the Middle East," *New Left Review*, no. 57 (1969).

2. Ibid.

3. Welty, "Palestinian Nationalism and the Struggle for National Self-Determination," pp. 18–24.

4. Rosemary Sayigh, *Palestinians: From Peasants to Revolutionaries* (London: Zed Press, 1979), pp. 98–143.

5. Nur Masalha, *Expulsion of the Palestinians* (Washington, D.C.: Institute for Palestine Studies, 1992), p. 175. Masalha goes on to point out: "The reasons of this mass exodus were categorized by the Israel

Defense Forces (IDF) Intelligence Branch as follows: Haganah/IDF operations ('at least 55 percent'); operations by IZL [Irgun Tzvai Leumi] and Lehi [Lohamei Herut Yisra'el] (15 percent); the whispering campaign psychological warfare, evacuation ordered by IDF, and general fear (14 percent)" (p. 179).

6. Ibid.

7. Ibid., p. 180.

8. Ben-Gurion, *Behilahem Yisrael* (As Israel fought) (Tel Aviv: Mapai Press, 1952), pp. 86–87, quoted in Masalha, *Expulsion of the Palestinians*, p. 181.

9. Quoted in Abdallah Frangi, *The PLO and Palestine* (London: Zed Books, 1983), p. 90.

10. Ibid., p. 89.

11. Ibid.

12. Chaliand, *Palestinian Resistance*, pp. 55–66.

13. Samir Amin, *The Arab Nation* (London: Zed Press, 1978). See also Roger Owen, "Arab Nationalism, Unity and Solidarity," in *The Middle East*, ed. Asad and Owen, pp. 18–19.

14. Joy Bonds et al., *Our Roots Are Still Alive* (San Francisco: People's Press, 1977), p. 111.

15. Ibid., pp. 111–12.

16. Gresh and Vidal, eds., *An A to Z of the Middle East*, pp. 207–8.

17. Sayigh, *Palestinians*, pp. 144–45.

18. Ibid., pp. 152–54.

19. Gresh and Vidal, eds., *An A to Z of the Middle East*, pp. 25–26.

20. Bonds et al., *Our Roots Are Still Alive*, p. 142.

21. Ibid.

22. Ibid., pp. 26–28.

23. Welty, "Palestinian Nationalism and the Struggle for National Self-Determination," pp. 25–32.

24. Gresh and Vidal, eds., *An A to Z of the Middle East*, p. 212.

25. Ibid., p. 213. See also B. J. Odeh, *Lebanon: Dynamics of Conflict* (London: Zed Press, 1985), pp. 197–202.

26. Estimates of the number of Palestinians massacred in the two camps vary from 700 to 3,500, with most sources documenting at least 1,300 massacred that are accounted for and more than 2,000 missing and presumed dead or buried in mass graves that have not been unearthed. See A. Frangi, *The PLO and Palestine* (London: Zed Books, 1983), pp. 222–39; Rosemary Sayigh, *Too Many Enemies: The Palestinian Experience in Lebanon* (London: Zed Books, 1994), p. 122. See also A. Kapeliouk, *Sabra and Shatila: Inquiry into a Massacre* (Belmont, Mass.: AAUG, 1984).

27. Frangi, *PLO and Palestine*, pp. 224–25; emphasis in the original.

28. Ibid., p. 225. The direct involvement of the Israeli high command in the planning and execution of the massacre is evidenced by the high-level meeting that took place between Israeli, Lebanese, and Falangist commanders to coordinate their efforts in accomplishing their mission: "At three o'clock that afternoon there was a meeting between Amos Yaron, commander of Israeli troops in Beirut, Fadi Ephram, supreme commander of the 'Lebanese Armed Forces' and Elias Hobeika, Ephram's secret police chief. They decided to carry out a 'mopping-up operation in the camp,' a move that had been planned for some time. The operation was to begin when darkness fell. Sharon gave his blessing over the telephone: 'My congratulations. The operation of our friends is approved.'" Ibid.

29. Ibid., p. 230.

30. Quoted in Frangi, *PLO and Palestine*, pp. 226–27.

31. Sayigh, *Too Many Enemies*, p. 121.

32. Ibid.

33. Ibid.

34. See Farideh Farhi, "Class Struggles, the State, and Revolution in Iran," in *Power and Stability in the Middle East*, ed. Berberoglu, pp. 90–113.

35. Andrew Rigby, *Living the Intifada* (London: Zed Books, 1991), p. 1.

36. F. Robert Hunter, *The Palestinian Uprising: A War by Other Means* (Berkeley: University of California Press, 1991), p. 58.

37. Ibid., pp. 59–60.

38. Ze'ev Schiff and Ehud Ya'ari, *Intifada: The Palestinian Uprising—Israel's Third Front* (New York: Simon and Schuster, 1990), p. 80.

39. Samih K. Farsoun and Jean M. Landis, "The Sociology of an Uprising: The Roots of the *Intifada*," in *Intifada: Palestine at the Crossroads*, ed. Jamal R. Nassar and Roger Heacock (New York: Praeger, 1990), p. 15.

40. David McDowall, *Palestine and Israel: The Uprising and Beyond* (Berkeley: University of California Press, 1989), p. 14.

41. Farsoun and Landis, "The Sociology of an Uprising," p. 16.

42. Zachary Lockman and Joel Beinin, *Intifada: The Palestinian Uprising Against Israeli Occupation* (Boston: South End Press, 1989).

43. F. Robert Hunter, *The Palestinian Uprising: A War By Other Means* (Berkeley: University of California Press, 1991), pp. 89–90.

44. Ibid., p. 90.

45. Ibid., p. 61.

Chapter 7. The Gulf War: Interimperialist Rivalry
for Control of Oil in the Middle East

1. For varied explanations on the nature and causes of the Gulf War of 1991, see *The Gulf War and the New World Order*, ed. Bresheeth and Yuval-Davis. See also Robert Brenner, "Why Is the United States at War with Iraq?" *New Left Review*, no. 185 (1991); Tom Mayer, "Imperialism and the Gulf War," *Monthly Review* 42, no. 11 (1991); Michael Tanzer, "Oil and the Gulf Crisis," *Monthly Review* 42, no. 11 (1991); Bernard D. Headley, "The 'New World Order' and the Persian Gulf War," *Humanity & Society* 15, no. 3 (1991); Edward Greer, "The Hidden History of the Iraq War," *Monthly Review* 43, no. 1. (1991); and Berch Berberoglu, "The Political Economy of the Gulf War," *Humanity & Society* 17, no. 1 (1993).

2. International Monetary Fund, *Direction of Trade Statistics, Yearbook 1970–76* (Washington, D.C.: IMF, 1977), pp. 148–49; *1982*, pp. 207–8; *1987*, pp. 229–30; *1991*, pp. 226–27.

3. Patrick Clawson, "The Internationalization of Capital and Capital Accumulation in Iran," in *Oil and Class Struggle*, ed. Peter Nore and Terisa Turner (London: Zed Press, 1980).

4. See Kaoru Sugihara, "Japan, the Middle East and the World Economy," in *Japan in the Contemporary Middle East*, ed. K. Sugihara and J. A. Allan (London: Routledge, 1993), pp. 1–13.

5. International Monetary Fund, *Direction of Trade Statistics, 1970–76*, pp. 150–51; *1982*, pp. 210–11; *1987*, pp. 231–32; *1991*, pp. 228–29.

6. Ibid., *1970–76*, pp. 148–49; *1982*, pp. 207–8; *1987*, pp. 229–30; *1991*, pp. 226–27.

7. Ibid., *1970–76*, pp. 148–49; *1982*, pp. 207–8; *1987*, pp. 229–30; *1991*, pp. 226–27.

8. Ibid., *1970–76*, pp. 150–51; *1982*, pp. 210–11; *1987*, pp. 231–32; *1991*, pp. 228–29.

9. Headley, "The 'New World Order' and the Persian Gulf War," p. 322.

10. Ibid., p. 323.

11. Ibid.

12. Quoted in Brenner, "Why Is the United States at War with Iraq?," p. 122.

13. Greer, "The Hidden History of the Iraq War," p. 6.

14. Ibid., pp. 6–7.

15. Ibid., p. 7.

16. Mayer, "Imperialism and the Gulf War," pp. 3–4.

17. Ibid., p. 4.

18. Ibid.

19. Japan was made to pay some $13 billion and Germany some $10 billion as part of "their share" of the cost of the war to secure *U.S.* victory! See Christopher Knowlton and Carla Rapoport, "Germany & Japan: Missing in Action," *Fortune*, 11 March 1991, p. 58.

20. See the *New York Times*, 28 March 1991, for a transcript of General Norman Schwarzkopf's interview "Talking With David Frost," in which the general said: "I would estimate . . . that we easily killed more than 100,000 [Iraqi soldiers]." Quoted in Greer, "The Hidden History of the Iraq War," p. 3.

Chapter 8. The Post–Cold War "New World Order" and the Prospects for Peace in the Middle East

1. Bresheeth and Yuval-Davis, eds., *The Gulf War and the New World Order*.

2. Ibid., pp. 24–28, 243–56.

3. Fawaz A. Gerges, *The Superpowers and the Middle East* (Boulder, Colo.: Westview Press, 1994); Peter Maugold, *Superpower Intervention in the Middle East* (New York: St. Martin's Press, 1978).

4. B. J. Odeh, *Lebanon: Dynamics of Conflict* (London: Zed Books, 1985).

5. Michael A. Attalides, *Cyprus: Nationalism and International Politics* (New York: St. Martin's Press, 1979), pp. 174–79. The Turkish invasion of Cyprus was a product of the U.S. policy of counterbalancing the power of two NATO allies in the region, Turkey and Greece. The United States intervened first in the internal affairs of Greece, through the CIA-led right-wing military coup that brought the generals to power in 1974; the generals then made moves to incorporate Cyprus into Greece. The United States then intervened in the internal affairs of Turkey by enticing the latter to respond to this challenge through the invasion of the island shortly thereafter. See Christopher Hitchens, *Cyprus* (New York: Quartet Books, 1984).

6. W. Thom Workman, *The Social Origins of the Iran-Iraq War* (Boulder, Colo.: Lynne Rienner, 1994). See also Dilip Hiro, *The Longest War: The Iran-Iraq Military Conflict* (London: Paladin, 1990).

7. Sami Yousif, "The Iraqi-U.S. War," in *The Gulf War and the New World Order*, ed. Bresheeth and Yural-Davis, pp. 62–68.

8. Bresheeth and Yuval-Davis, eds., *The Gulf War and the New World Order*. For an analysis of the U.S. role in interimperialist rivalry

for control of oil in this most recent phase of Great Power politics in the Middle East, see chapter 7 in this book.

9. Odeh, *Lebanon: Dynamics of Conflict*, pp. 131–72, 189–208.

10. David McDowall, *Lebanon: A Conflict of Minorities* (London: Minority Rights Group, 1985), p. 16.

11. Michael Jansen, *The Battle of Beirut: Why Israel Invaded Lebanon* (London: Zed Press, 1982).

12. Odeh, *Lebanon: Dynamics of Conflict*, pp. 173–86.

13. Ibid.

14. David McDowall, *The Kurds: A Nation Denied* (London: Minority Rights Publications, 1992).

15. Andrew Rigby, *Living the Intifada* (London: Zed Books, 1991). See also Adel Samara et al., *Palestine: Profile of an Occupation* (London: Zed Books, 1989).

BIBLIOGRAPHY

Abdullah, Samir. 1996. *The Middle East Peace Dilemma*. Cairo: Economic Research Forum.

Aburish, Said K. 1996. *The Rise, Corruption, and Coming Fall of the House of Saud*. New York: St. Martin's Press.

Aksoy, S. 1971. *Türkiye'de Toprak Meselesi* (The land question in Turkey). Istanbul: Gerçek Yayinevi.

Alnasrawi, Abbas. 1994. "Economic Devastation, Underdevelopment and Outlook." In *Iraq Since the Gulf War*, edited by Fran Hazelton. London: Zed Books.

Amin, Samir. 1978. *The Arab Nation: Nationalism and Class Struggles*. London: Zed Press.

Arpee, L. 1909. *The Armenian Awakening, 1820–1860*. Chicago: University of Chicago Press.

Aruri, Nasser, ed. 1986. *Occupation: Israel Over Palestine*. Boulder, Colo.: Westview Press.

Asad, Talal, and Roger Owen, eds. 1983. *The Middle East*. New York: Monthly Review Press.

Attalides, Michael A. 1979. *Cyprus: Nationalism and International Politics*. New York: St. Martin's Press.

Azim, Ahmad N. 1989. "Egypt: The Origins and Development of a Neo-colonial State." In *Power and Stability in the Middle East*, edited by Berch Berberoglu. London: Zed Books.

Bassam, Tibi. 1988. *The Crisis of Modern Islam: A Preindustrial Culture in the Scientific-Technological Age*. Translated by Judith von Sivers. Salt Lake City: University of Utah Press.

Batatu, Hanna. 1978. *The Old Social Classes and the Revolutionary Movements in Iraq*. Princeton: Princeton University Press.

147

Bayat, Asef. 1996. "The Coming of a Post-Islamist Society." *Critique,* no. 9 (Fall).

Beattie, Kirk J. 1994. *Egypt During the Nasser Years.* Boulder, Colo.: Westview Press.

Beinin, Joel. 1982. "Egypt's Transition Under Nasser." *MERIP Reports* 107 (July/August).

Bendt, Ingela, and James Downing. 1982. *We Shall Return: Women of Palestine.* London: Zed Press.

Berberoglu, Berch. 1982. *Turkey in Crisis: From State Capitalism to Neo-Colonialism.* London: Zed Books.

———. 1987. *The Internationalization of Capital: Imperialism and Capitalist Development on a World Scale.* New York: Praeger.

———. 1992. *The Political Economy of Development: Development Theory and the Prospects for Change in the Third World.* Albany: State University of New York Press.

———, ed. 1989. *Power and Stability in the Middle East.* London: Zed Books.

———, ed. 1995. *The National Question: Nationalism, Ethnic Conflict and Self-Determination in the Twentieth Century.* Philadelphia, Pa.: Temple University Press.

Berkes, Niyazi. 1964. *The Development of Secularism in Turkey* Montreal: McGill University Press.

Besikçi, Ismail. 1988. *Kurdistan: An Interstate Colony.* Sydney: Australian Kurdish Association.

———. 1991. *The State of Terror in the Middle East.* Ankara: Yurt Kitap Yayinlari.

Bina, Cyrus, and Hamid Zangeneh, eds. 1992. *Modern Capitalism and Islamic Ideology in Iran.* New York: St. Martin's Press.

Blaisdell, D. C. 1929. *European Financial Control in the Ottoman Empire.* New York: Columbia University Press.

Bonds, Joy, et al. 1977. *Our Roots Are Still Alive.* San Francisco: People's Press.

Boyarin, Jonathan. 1996. *Palestine and Jewish History.* Minneapolis: University of Minnesota Press.

Braude, Benjamin, and Bernard Lewis, eds. 1982. *Christians and Jews in the Ottoman Empire.* New York: Holmes & Meier.

Brenner, Robert. 1991. "Why Is the United States at War with Iraq?" *New Left Review,* no. 185.

Bresheeth, Haim, and Nira Yuval-Davis, eds. 1991. *The Gulf War and the New World Order.* London: Zed Books.

Bruinessen, Martin van. 1992. *Agha, Shaikh, and State: The Social and Political Structures of Kurdistan.* London: Zed Books.

Çavdar, T. 1970. *Osmanlilarin Yari-Sömürge Olusu* (The semicolonization of the Ottomans). Istanbul: Ant Yayinlari.

Chaliand, Gerard. 1972. *The Palestinian Resistance*. Baltimore, Md.: Penguin.

———. 1980. *People Without a Country: The Kurds and Kurdistan*. London: Zed Books.

———. 1994. *The Kurdish Tragedy*. London: Zed Books.

Chaliand, Gerard, and Yves Ternon. 1983. *The Armenians: From Genocide to Resistance*. London: Zed Books.

Ciment, James. 1996. *The Kurds: State and Minority in Turkey, Iraq and Iran*. New York: Facts On File.

Clawson, Patrick. 1980. "The Internationalization of Capital and Capital Accumulation in Iran." In *Oil and Class Struggle*, edited by Petter Nore and Terisa Turner. London: Zed Press.

Cleveland, William L. 1993. *A History of the Modern Middle East*. Boulder, Colo.: Westview Press.

Cobban, Helena. 1984. *The Palestinian Liberation Organization*. Cambridge: Cambridge University Press.

Committee Against Repression and for Democratic Rights in Iraq (CARDRI), eds. 1994. *Saddam's Iraq: Revolution or Reaction?* London: Zed Books.

Cooley, John. 1973. *Green March, Black September*. London: Frank Cass.

Cooper, Mark. 1983. "Egyptian State Capitalism in Crisis." In *The Middle East*, edited by Talal Asad and Roger Owen. New York: Monthly Review Press.

Dadrian, Vahakn N. 1986. "The Naim-Andonian Documents on the World War I Destruction of Ottoman Armenians: The Anatomy of a Genocide." *International Journal of Middle East Studies* 18:311–60.

———. 1989. "Genocide as a Problem of National and International Law: The World War I Armenian Case and Its Contemporary Legal Ramifications." *The Yale Journal of International Law* 14, no. 2 (Summer): 221–78.

———. 1995. *The History of the Armenian Genocide*. Providence, R.I.: Berghahn Books.

Eagleton, William, Jr. 1963. *The Kurdish Republic of 1946*. London: Oxford University Press.

Earle, Edward Mead. 1966. *Turkey, the Great Powers, and the Bagdad Railway: A Study in Imperialism*. New York: Russell & Russell.

Eickelman, Dale. 1989. *The Middle East: An Anthropological Approach*. Englewood Cliffs, N.J.: Prentice-Hall.

Emadi, Hafizullah. 1990. *State, Revolution and Superpowers in Afghanistan*. New York: Praeger.

Ergil, Dogu. 1975. "From Empire to Dependence: The Evolution of Turkish Underdevelopment." Ph.D. diss., State University of New York at Binghamton.

Farhi, Farideh. 1989. "Class Struggles, the State, and Revolution in Iran." In *Power and Stability in the Middle East*, edited by Berch Berberoglu. London: Zed Books.

Farouk-Sluglett, Marion, and Peter Sluglett. 1987. *Iraq Since 1958: From Revolution to Dictatorship*. London: KPI.

———. 1991. "The Social Classes and the Origins of the Revolution." In *The Iraqi Revolution of 1958*, edited by Robert A. Fernea and Wm. Roger Louis. New York: I. B. Tauris.

Farsoun, Samih. 1982. "Israel's Goal of Destroying the PLO is Not Achievable." *Journal of Palestine Studies* 11, no. 4.

Farsoun, Samih, and Christina Zacharia. 1997. *Palestine and the Palestinians*. Boulder, Colo.: Westview Press.

Farsoun, Samih, and Jean M. Landis. 1990. "The Sociology of an Uprising: The Roots of the Intifada." In *Intifada: Palestine at the Crossroads*, edited by Jamal R. Nassar and Roger Heacock. New York: Praeger.

Finch, E. A. 1957. "Social Effects of the Oil Industry in Iraq." *International Labour Review*, March.

Finkelstein, Norman G. 1996. *The Rise and Fall of Palestine: A Personal Account of the Intifada Years*. Minneapolis: University of Minnesota Press.

Foran, John, ed. 1994. *A Century of Revolution: Social Movements in Iran*. Minneapolis: University of Minnesota Press.

Frangi, Abdallah. 1983. *The PLO and Palestine*. London: Zed Books.

Genet, Jean. 1983. "Four Hours in Shatila." *Journal of Palestine Studies* 12, no. 2.

Gerges, Fawaz. 1994. *The Superpowers and the Middle East*. Boulder, Colo.: Westview Press.

Ghareeb, Edmund. 1981. *The Kurdish Question in Iraq*. Syracuse, N.Y.: Syracuse University Press.

Ghassemlou, Abdul Rahman. 1965. *Kurdistan and the Kurds*. London: Collets Holdings.

Goldberg, Ellis Jay. 1996. *The Social History of Labor in the Middle East*. Boulder, Colo.: Westview Press.

Greer, Edward. 1991. "The Hidden History of the Iraq War." *Monthly Review* 43, no. 1.

Gresh, Alain. 1985. *The PLO: The Struggle Within*. London: Zed Books.

Gresh, Alain, and Dominique Vidal, ed. 1990. *An A to Z of the Middle East*. London: Zed Books.

Gunter, Michael M. 1991. *The Kurds in Turkey: A Political Dilemma.* Westport, Conn.: Greenwood Press.

Halliday, Fred. 1975. *Arabia Without Sultans.* New York: Vintage.

————. 1996. *Islam and the Myth of Confrontation: Religion and Politics in the Middle East.* London: I. B. Tauris.

Halliday, Fred, and Hamza Alavi, eds. 1988. *The State and Ideology in the Middle East and Pakistan.* New York: Monthly Review Press.

Hazelton, Fran, ed. 1994. *Iraq Since the Gulf War.* London: Zed Books.

Headley, Bernard D. 1991. "The 'New World Order' and the Persian Gulf War." *Humanity & Society* 15, no. 3.

Hiro, Dilip. 1996. *A Dictionary of the Middle East.* New York: St. Martin's Press.

Hitchens, Christopher. 1984. *Cyprus.* New York: Quartet Books.

Hopwood, Derek. 1988. *Syria, 1945–1986: Politics and Society.* London: Unwin Hyman.

Hourani, A. H. 1946. *Syria and Lebanon: A Political Essay* London: RIIA.

Hovannisian, Richard G. 1978. *The Armenian Holocaust.* Cambridge, Mass.: Armenian Heritage Press.

————. 1987. *The Armenian Genocide in Perspective.* New Brunswick, N.J.: Transaction Books.

Hunter, F. Robert. 1991. *The Palestinian Uprising: A War By Other Means.* Berkeley: University of California Press.

Hurewitz, J. C. 1968. *The Struggle for Palestine.* New York: Greenwood Press.

Hussain, Mahmoud. 1973. *Class Conflict in Egypt, 1945–1970.* New York: Monthly Review Press.

Ibrahim, Ferhad. 1995. "The Kurdish National Movement and the Struggle for National Autonomy." In *The National Question: Nationalism, Ethnic Conflict, and Self Determination in the Twentieth Century,* edited by Berch Berberoglu. Philadelphia, Pa.: Temple University Press.

Islamoglu-Inan, Huri, ed. 1987. *The Ottoman Empire and the World Economy.* Cambridge: Cambridge University Press.

Issawi, Charles. 1980. *The Economic History of Turkey, 1800–1914.* Chicago: University of Chicago Press.

————. 1982. *The Economic History of the Middle East and North Africa.* New York: Columbia University Press.

Jansen, Michael. 1982. *The Battle of Beirut: Why Israel Invaded Lebanon.* London: Zed Press.

————. 1987. *Dissonance in Zion.* London: Zed Books.

Kadri, Ali. 1996. "Social Transformation in the West Bank." *Critique,* no. 8 (Spring).

Kapeliouk, A. 1984. *Sabra and Shatila: Inquiry into a Massacre.* Belmont, Mass.: AAUG.

Karpat, Kemal H. 1978. "Ottoman Population Records and the Census of 1881/82–1893." *International Journal of Middle East Studies* 9:237–74.

———. 1985. *Ottoman Population, 1830–1914: Demographic and Social Characteristics.* Madison: University of Wisconsin Press.

Kasaba, Resat. 1988. *The Ottoman Empire and the World Economy.* Albany: State University of New York Press.

Kashi, Ed. 1994. *When the Borders Bleed: The Struggle of the Kurds.* New York: Pantheon Books.

Kedourie, Elie. 1988. "Great Britain, the Other Powers, and the Middle East Before and After World War I." In *The Great Powers in the Middle East, 1919–1939,* edited by Uriel Dann. New York: Holmes & Maier.

Keyder, Çaglar. 1981. *The Definition of a Peripheral Economy: Turkey, 1923–1929.* Cambridge: Cambridge University Press.

———. 1987. *State and Class in Turkey: A Study in Capitalist Development.* London: Verso.

Khadduri, Majid. 1969. *Republican Iraq.* London: Oxford University Press.

Khalidi, Rashid, et al., eds. 1991. *The Origins of Arab Nationalism.* New York: Columbia University Press.

Khoury, Nabil F., and Valentine M. Moghadam, eds. 1995. *Gender and Development in the Arab World.* London: Zed Books.

Khoury, Philip S. 1987. *Syria and the French Mandate: The Politics of Arab Nationalism, 1920–1945.* Princeton: Princeton University Press.

Kimmerling, Baruch, and Joel S. Migdal. 1993. *Palestinians: The Making of A People.* New York: The Free Press.

Knowlton, Christopher, and Carla Rapoport. 1991. "Germany and Japan: Missing in Action." *Fortune,* 11 March.

Kreyenbroek, Philip G., and Stefan Sperl, eds. 1992. *The Kurds: A Contemporary Overview.* London: Routledge.

Krikorian, Mesrob K. 1977. *Armenians in the Service of the Ottoman Empire, 1860–1908.* London: Routledge & Kegan Paul.

Kuper, Leo. 1982. *Genocide: Its Political Use in the Twentieth Century.* New Haven: Yale University Press.

Langer, William L. 1935. *The Diplomacy of Imperialism, 1890–1902.* Vol. 1. New York: Alfred A. Knopf.

Langley, Kathleen. 1961. *The Industrialization of Iraq.* Cambridge: Harvard University Press.

Lawson, Fred H. 1989. "Class Politics and State Power in Ba'thi Syria."

In *Power and Stability in the Middle East*, edited by Berch Berberoglu. London: Zed Books.

Lazarev, M. S. 1980. *Kurdistan i Kurdskaia Problema*. Reprinted in *Economic History of Turkey*, by Charles Issawi. Chicago: University of Chicago Press. Original edition, Moscow: Nauka, 1964.

Lesch, David W. 1996. *The Middle East and the United States: A Historical and Political Reassessment*. Boulder, Colo.: Westview Press.

Lewis, Bernard. 1969. *The Emergence of Modern Turkey*. 2d ed. New York: Oxford University Press.

———. 1994. *The Shaping of the Modern Middle East*. New York: Oxford University Press.

———. 1995. *The Middle East: A Brief History of the Last Two Thousand Years*. New York: Scribner.

Lockman, Zachary, and Joel Beinin. 1989. *Intifada: The Palestinian Uprising Against Israeli Occupation*. Boston: South End Press.

Longuenesse, Elizabeth. 1979. "The Class Nature of the State in Syria." *MERIP Reports* 9, no. 4 (May).

Louis, William Roger. 1988. *The British Empire in the Middle East: 1945–1951*. Oxford: Clarendon Press.

Mansfield, Peter. 1965. *Nasser's Egypt*. Baltimore, Md.: Penguin.

Mansour, Fawzy. 1992. *The Arab World*. London: Zed Books.

Masalha, Nur. 1992. *Expulsion of the Palestinians*. Washington, D.C.: Institute for Palestine Studies.

Mayer, Tom. 1991. "Imperialism and the Gulf War." *Monthly Review* 42, no. 11.

McBride, Sean. 1988. *Israel in Lebanon*. London: Ithaca Press.

McCarthy, Justin. 1983. *Muslims and Minorities: The Population of Ottoman Anatolia and the End of the Empire*. New York: New York University Press.

McDowall, David. 1989. *Palestine and Israel: The Uprising and Beyond*. Berkeley: University of California Press.

———. 1992. *The Kurds: A Nation Denied*. London: Minority Rights Group.

———. 1995. *The Palestinians: The Road to Nationhood*. London: Minority Rights Group.

———. 1996. *A Modern History of the Kurds*. London: I. B. Tauris.

Melson, Robert. 1982. "A Theoretical Inquiry into the Armenian Massacres of 1894–1896." *Comparative Studies in Society and History* 24, no. 3 (July): 481–509.

Moaddel, Mansoor. 1993. *Class, Politics and Ideology in the Iranian Revolution*. New York: Columbia University Press.

Moghadam, Valentine M. 1994. *Gender and National Identity: Women and Politics in Muslim Societies*. London: Zed Books.

Murphy, Emma C. 1996. "The Arab-Israeli Peace Process." *Critique,* no. 9 (Fall).

Nahla, Zu'bbi. 1986. "The Development of Capitalism in Palestine." *Journal of Palestine Studies* 13.

Nalbandian, Louise. 1967. *The Armenian Revolutionary Movement.* Berkeley: University of California Press.

Nassibian, Akaby. 1984. *Britain and the Armenian Question, 1915–1923.* New York: St. Martin's Press.

Niblock, Tim. 1982. Introduction to *Iraq: The Contemporary State,* edited by Tim Niblock. New York: St. Martin's Press.

Odeh, B. J. 1985. *Lebanon: Dynamics of Conflict.* London: Zed Press.

Olson, Robert, ed. 1996. *The Kurdish Nationalist Movement in the 1990s.* Lexington: The University Press of Kentucky.

Owen, Roger. 1992. *State, Power and Politics in the Making of the Modern Middle East.* London: Routledge.

Paul, Jim. 1982. "Foreign Investment in Egypt." *MERIP Reports* 107 (July/August).

Peretz, Don. 1990. *Intifada: The Palestinian Uprising.* Boulder, Colo.: Westview Press.

Permanent Peoples' Tribunal. 1985. *A Crime of Silence: The Armenian Genocide.* London: Zed Books.

Perry, Glenn E., ed. 1986. *Palestine: Continuing Dispossession.* Belmont, Mass.: Association of Arab-American University Graduates.

Peteet, Julie M. 1991. *Gender in Crisis: Women and the Palestinian Resistance Movement.* New York: Columbia University Press.

Petran, Tabitha. 1972. *Syria.* New York: Praeger.

———. 1987. *The Struggle Over Lebanon.* New York: Monthly Review Press.

Qubain, Fahim. 1958. *The Reconstruction of Iraq, 1950–57.* New York: Praeger.

Rahnema, Saeed, and Sohrab Behdad, eds. 1996. *Iran After the Revolution: Crisis of an Islamic State.* London: I. B. Tauris.

Ramazanoglu, Hüseyin, ed. 1985. *Turkey in the World Capitalist System.* Aldershot, U.K.: Gower.

Ramsaur, E. E. 1965. *The Young Turks: Prelude to the Revolution of 1908.* Beirut: Khayat.

Reilly, James. 1982. "Israel in Lebanon, 1975–82." *MERIP Reports* 12, nos. 6–7 (September–October).

Rigby, Andrew. 1991. *Living the Intifada.* London: Zed Books.

Rodinson, Maxime. 1987. *Europe and the Mystique of Islam.* Seattle: University of Washington Press.

Saba, Paul. 1989. "The Armenian National Question." In *Power and Stability in the Middle East*, edited by Berch Berberoglu. London: Zed Books.

Said, Edward W. 1994. *The Politics of Dispossession: The Struggle for Palestinian Self-Determination, 1969–1994.* New York: Pantheon.

Sarc, O. C. 1966. "Ottoman Industrial Policy, 1840–1914." In *The Economic History of the Middle East, 1800–1914*, edited by Charles Issawi. Chicago: University of Chicago Press.

Sayigh, Rosemary. 1979. *Palestinians: From Peasants to Revolutionaries.* London: Zed Press.

———. 1994. *Too Many Enemies: The Palestinian Experience in Lebanon.* London: Zed Books.

Schiff, Ze'ev, and Ehud Ya'ari. 1990. *Intifada: The Palestinian Uprising—Israel's Third Front.* New York: Simon and Schuster.

Shoukri, Ghali. 1981. *Egypt: Portrait of a President.* London: Zed Press.

Sid-Ahmed, Mohamed. 1991. "The Gulf Crisis and the New World Order." *Middle East Report*, January–February.

Smith, Pamela Ann. 1989. "Palestine and the Palestinians." In *Power and Stability in the Middle East*, edited by Berch Berberoglu. London: Zed Books.

Stivers, William. 1982. *Supremacy and Oil: Iraq, Turkey, and the Anglo-American World Order, 1918–1930.* Ithaca: Cornell University Press.

Stork, Joe. 1975. *Middle East Oil and the Energy Crisis.* New York: Monthly Review Press.

———. 1981. "Iraq and the War in the Gulf." *MERIP Reports* 97 (June).

Sugihara, Kaoru, and J. A. Allan, eds. 1993. *Japan in the Contemporary Middle East.* London: Routledge.

Tamari, Salim. 1982. "Factionalism and Class Formation in Recent Palestinian History." In *Studies in the Economic and Social History of Palestine in the Nineteenth and Twentieth Centuries*, edited by Roger Owen. London: Macmillan.

Tanzer, Michael. 1991. "Oil and the Gulf Crisis." *Monthly Review* 42, no. 11.

Tapper, Richard, ed. 1983. *The Conflict of Tribe and State in Iran and Afghanistan.* London: Croom-Helm.

Taylan, Turgut. 1984. "Capital and the State in Contemporary Turkey." *Khamsin*, no. 11.

Tessler, Mark. 1994. *A History of the Israeli-Palestinian Conflict.* Bloomington: Indiana University Press.

Tripp, Charles, and Roger Owens, eds. 1989. *Egypt Under Mubarak.* London: Routledge.

U.S. Office of Naval Intelligence. 1923. *The United States Navy as an Industrial Asset*. Washington, D.C.: ONI.

Usakligil, Halit Ziya. 1936. *Kirk Yil*. 5 vols. Excerpted in *Economic History of Turkey*, by Charles Issawi. Chicago: University of Chicago Press.

Vali, Abbas. 1996. "The Making of Kurdish Identity in Iran." *Critique*, no. 7 (Fall).

Walker, Christopher J. 1980. *Armenia: The Survival of a Nation*. New York: St. Martin's Press.

Welty, Gordon. 1995. "Palestinian Nationalism and the Struggle for National Self-Determination." In *The National Question: Nationalism, Ethnic Conflict and Self-Determination in the Twentieth Century*, edited by Berch Berberoglu. Philadelphia, Pa.: Temple University Press.

Whiting, Richard C. 1983. "The Suez Canal and the British Economy 1918–1960." In *Imperialism and Nationalism in the Middle East*, edited by Keith M. Wilson. London: Mansell.

Wiener, Jon. 1991. "Domestic Political Incentives for the Gulf War." *New Left Review*, no. 187.

Workman, W. Thom. 1994. *The Social Origins of the Iran-Iraq War*. Boulder, Colo.: Lynne Rienner.

Van Dam, Nikolaos. 1979. *The Struggle for Power in Syria*. New York: St. Martin's Press.

Vanly, Ismet Sheriff. 1971. *Survey of the National Question of Turkish Kurdistan with Historical Background*. Zurich: Hevra.

Yergin, Daniel. 1991. *The Prize: The Epic Quest for Oil, Money, and Power*. New York: Simon & Schuster.

Zaher, U. 1989. "Political Developments in Iraq 1963–1980." In *Saddam's Iraq: Revolution or Reaction?*, edited by Committee Against Repression and for Democratic Rights in Iraq (CARDRI). London: Zed Books.

Zoryan Institute. 1997. *Problems of Genocide*. Toronto: Zoryan Institute of Canada.

ABOUT THE AUTHOR

Dr. Berch Berberoglu is Foundation Professor, chairman of the Department of Sociology, and director of the Institute for International Studies at the University of Nevada, Reno, where he has been teaching and conducting research for the past twenty-two years. He is the author and editor of sixteen books and many articles on the Middle East, the global political economy, class structure, and related macrosociological topics. His recent books include *The National Question: Nationalism, Ethnic Conflict and Self-Determination in the Twentieth Century* (Temple University Press, 1995) and *Class Structure and Social Transformation* (Praeger, 1994). He is currently writing a new book, entitled *Class, State, and Nation: The Class Nature of Nationalism and Ethnic Conflict*, which will be published by Greenwood Press in 2000.

INDEX